Authority:

The Critical Issue
for Southern Baptists

BY JAMES T. DRAPER, JR.

Discover Joy
Ecclesiastes, the Life without God
Faith that Works
Foundations of Biblical Faith
Hebrews, the Life that Pleases God
Jonah, Living in Rebellion
Live Up to Your Faith
Proverbs, the Secret of Beautiful Living
Say Neighbor, Your House Is on Fire
The Church Christ Approves
The Conscience of a Nation
Titus, Patterns for Church Living
What to Do till the Lord Comes
Authority: The Critical Issue for Southern Baptists

Authority:
The Critical Issue for Southern Baptists

DR. JAMES T. DRAPER, JR.
Foreword by Herschel H. Hobbs

Fleming H. Revell Company
Old Tappan, New Jersey

Library of Congress Cataloging in Publication Data

Draper, James T.
Authority: the critical issue for Southern Baptists.

Includes bibliographical references.
1. Bible—Evidences, authority, etc.   2. Southern Baptist Convention—Doctrines.   3. Baptists—Doctrines.
I. Title.
BS480.D72   1984   220.1'3   83-19143
ISBN 0-8007-1389-3

Contents

5

Introduction

We in the church today face a crisis of authority. We acknowledge Jesus Christ as Lord of the church, but we ask: How does He exercise His authority in the earth today? As Christians, what is our rule of faith and order? This issue confronts virtually every communion and denomination within the Body of Christ and is a chief concern of the people and churches making up the Southern Baptist Convention.

Southern Baptists are conservative theologically. We have always sought our authority in the Bible and have justly deserved to be called "people of the Book." But due to human frailty, we do not all interpret the Bible alike. Some are more conservative than others. Some take more liberties than do others. Both these camps—sometimes called "moderates" and "fundamentalists," or "liberals" and "conservatives"—have become more visible in recent years in the debate over authority.

James Draper, claiming friendship with people on both sides of the present difference in doctrine, avowed when he became president of the convention, that he *belonged* to neither side. No man in my memory has worked harder than he has to bridge this difference. Drawing upon his widespread friendships, he has brought together people prominently identified with each side—if not to full agreement—at least to talk with one another.

"Jimmy," as he is affectionately called, has written this present volume, *Authority: The Critical Issue for Southern Baptists,* to set forth some basic steps toward solving the current differences. While specific in his pronouncements, he allows for those differences which are inherent in our Baptist polity and practice.

As Mission Control periodically corrects the course of NASA space vehicles, to direct them toward a destination, so President Draper is calling on us to withstand the forces that would draw us off our God-appointed path. This book follows in the tradition of The Baptist Faith and Message adopted by our convention in 1925 and revised in 1963. It is the much-needed corrective to keep Southern Baptists on target in evangelism and missions worldwide. Herein, President Draper has charted a course which all of us can follow. Let us read and ponder the message, the *plea* of this book. Then, in the spirit of the author, our chosen leader, let us unite hearts and hands as we move toward the goal dear to all our hearts—reaching the world with the saving gospel of the Lord Jesus Christ.

Herschel H. Hobbs
Former President, Southern Baptist Convention
Pastor Emeritus, First Baptist Church
Oklahoma City, Oklahoma

Preface

These pages are written out of a deep concern for the people called Southern Baptists, in particular, and the Christian community in general. I must declare at the very outset that these pages are only one man's attempt to cast some understanding on a controversy that has generated more heat than light in recent years. This controversy revolves around the issue of authority.

First, however, may I say that these pages are written in love and with a keen understanding that only as we approach each other in love can we resolve critical issues such as the one before us. Second, let us note that we cannot demand absolute conformity among ourselves in order for us to work and worship together. If we are God's people—saved through faith in our Lord Jesus Christ—then we have a foundation and a basis for serving God and one another. Third, I ask you to read this in its entirety before making a final judgment on its value and propositions.

I believe the key issue among Southern Baptists, and, for that matter, all Christian people today is the matter of AUTHORITY. Where does genuine authority come from? Who or what is the source of our authority? Is there a standard, a "rule" which will be authoritative for God's people today? Daily the church faces ongoing issues that demand answers. Inevitably, the answer or lack of answer relates to authority. It has become the critical issue of our times.

There are some in the church who appeal to their denominational heritage as their authority. Others rely upon the authority of educational achievement. There are those who claim authority based upon their proven intellectual powers. Still others claim the authority based on the practice of our churches and conventions. If enough of us are doing it or claiming it, they say, then it must be correct. And there are many other potential sources for claiming the right to believe or act in a particular manner.

From my perspective, although many of these sources of authority have legitimacy in various areas of life, underlying all of them must be the one unchanging yet dynamically relevant authority, namely, the Word of God. The Scriptures must be the final ground for guidance in all arenas of life. This raises other issues. Is the Bible truth without error, or is it a book that only contains truth? Since man was uniquely involved in its delivery, is it woven both within and without with error and imperfections?

My purpose in this book is to examine the key issues that face us as they relate to the Word of God. We will explore epistemology—how we know what we know, how we perceive truth, and how we determine that a document such as the Bible is truth without error.

Next, we will consider the three possible foundations for ultimate authority for mankind. These, as we shall see, are rationalism or reason, ecclesiastical fiat, and divine revelation in the Bible. To understand how Southern Baptists have arrived at this crucial point in the controversy over authority, we will look at four rather modern developments and see how they affect modern theological thought:

1) The historical-critical approach to Scripture,

2) The rise of existential philosophy,

3) The impact of naturalistic and uniformitarian science, and

4) The presumed contributions of major world religions.

As we consider these we will observe the manner in which many in the church have shifted from divine revelation to rationalism as their ultimate base of authority. This tragic shift has led us into religious experience without theological foundation, situational ethics without absolutes, and evangelism without an adequate biblical concept of man's lost condition.

An essential part in determining the critical issue facing Southern Baptists will be a review of what church leaders through the centuries have believed with regard to authority. We will also look at the developing history of our own Southern Baptist Convention to discover what the early founders and leaders believed about the authority of Scripture. It is very important for us to know our heritage. Without that, the issue today would be meaningless.

We will see what the Bible says about itself and study the meaning of biblical inspiration. This book is *not* about inerrancy or inspiration. It is about authority. Inerrancy and inspiration are related topics, but they are not the critical issue.

Finally, we will address ourselves to the future. Where do we go from here? I have said that to work together it is not necessary that we be conformed absolutely to one viewpoint; but there must be limits beyond which we cannot go. We will endeavor to suggest the direction that must be taken if we are to remain a vital, aggressive part of the Lord's work in this world.

This book is a labor of love. I am committed to serving our Lord through our Southern Baptist Convention, and I ask that these pages be received in the context of my love and my commitment within the framework of our Southern Baptist Convention.

James T. Draper, Jr.

Authority:

The Critical Issue
for Southern Baptists

CHAPTER 1

A Tragic Step That Can Lead to Spiritual Disaster

"There are people among us today, teaching in our institutions, laboring in our denomination, pastoring in our churches, who have not departed all that far from classic biblical doctrine. They still believe that Jesus is God. They still believe in the bodily resurrection of Christ. They still believe in the virgin birth. But, they do not believe that everything in Scripture is necessarily accurate and without error. They have started over the edge."

THE CHRISTIAN COMMUNITY in recent years has taken a tragic step in its theological commitment. Sometimes consciously, sometimes subconsciously, but always tragically, many professing Christians have slowly moved away from the historic position concerning the nature of the Bible. Little or large, deliberate or not, when one takes such a step he courts disaster in his life and ministry. When one takes that tragic step the result is usually a loss of mission and evangelistic zeal; theological defection; undue emphasis upon the material and temporal with a corresponding loss of consciousness of the eternal; reliance upon mystical, personal experience instead of revealed truth; unjustified attachment to human reasoning—to name but a few spiritually-destructive positions.

The basic problem which we face today has to do with knowledge and truth. It is not the *quantity* of truth which is being debated, but the *source* of truth. Where does genuine truth originate, and how can we know that something is actually truth? This is the burning issue challenging every serious Bible student and Christian today. Philosophically, we refer to this whole area of study as epistemology.

Epistemology has to do with how we know what we know and how we know what is true. The word *epistemology* comes from the Greek verb *epistomai,* which means "to know" or "to understand." This is very basic to the whole discussion concerning the problem in modern theology because it brings us to the question of ultimate authority. How can we analyze the competing claims to truth? There are three basic possibilities. These three possibilities are (1) human reason or rationalism, (2) ecclesiastical authority, and (3) divine revelation.

I use the term *rationalism* as an umbrella term. In the classical sense, rationalism, as evidenced by the so-called rationalistic philosophers, means that there is innately or naturally within man's mind the capability of knowing truth. This view holds that man has the intrinsic ability to put together facts and arrive at valid conclusions. What I really mean by this term, however, is not only classic rationalism, but also classic empiricism. This is the idea that truth can be determined by experimentation, by our sense, by our observation of phenomena.

For our purposes, these two fall basically under the same category. This is because whether we believe that ultimate truth is a product of what goes on in our minds instinctively or whether it is something put into our minds by what we see, experience, or experiment with, all of it still comes down to a matter of one's own personal mind, reason, and experience as being the ultimate determination of truth.

We also include under this category of rationalism the idea of mysticism. This is the concept that somehow truth pops into our minds through some mystical experience, which "truth" we then can use to analyze and evaluate phenomena. Taken together, all of these still constitute the human mind as ultimate authority, whether it be by intrinsic ability, mystical infiltration, or experimentation and sense experience. All of these processes bring the human mind ultimately to the forefront as the ultimate source of authority. Whatever, then, is to be evaluated as true or false must pass through the filter of my own mind, my own intelligence. Whether it be instinctively perceived, informed by experimentation and observation, or informed by some presumed mystical experience, it is, nonetheless, what I think that ultimately determines what is true.

The second basic possibility for determining what is true is ecclesiastical authority. This is not quite so confusing and is easier to handle. This, in effect, says that my church is ultimate authority. Regardless of whether I think something is right or not, if the church says it is right, then it is right for me. Regardless of any other aspect of authority, the church is my ultimate authority. The classic example, of course, would be the Roman Catholic Church. The faithful within the Roman Church are supposed to receive the dogma of the church as being of God, as being absolute and final truth. Even Scripture is subservient to ecclesiastical authority, because, according to the Roman Church, the Bible is the product of the church. Mother church produced even the Scriptures, and, although they claim that Scripture does not contradict the dogma of the church, nonetheless, even if it did, church authority would prevail because the church is the mother of Scripture. So, ultimately and finally, what is right and wrong, what is true and false, is determined by

what the church officially has determined through its pronouncements.

The third possible basis of authority is divine revelation.
This actually falls into two areas—general or natural revelation which is the revelation of God in His creation, and special revelation, which is the Word of God. Today this means
Scripture, since the biblical writers are no longer on the
scene. We do not believe that Scripture is still being written
today.

Here we have the three possible bases of ultimate authority. Though most people do not stop to consider it, everyone operates from one of these bases. For example,
Martin Luther said, "My conscience is captive to the Word
of God." That means that when I think one thing, but the
Bible says something else, then the Bible is true and my
thinking is false, and I must adjust my thinking to what the
Bible declares. Luther was operating from the base of divine
revelation.

Anytime a person says, "I do not believe the Bible is correct at this point," he is operating from the base of rationalism or human reason. The very fact that he regards the
Bible as incorrect indicates in itself that he has some authority which transcends the Bible. We cannot correct something unless we have something which is more accurate,
more nearly true, more authoritative, than the thing which
we are correcting. So, any time a person says that he finds
any supposed flaw or untruth in Scripture, something which
would tend to militate against its accuracy, he has demonstrated by that statement that he has a higher basis of authority than Scripture. Presumably, it could be either
ecclesiastical authority or rationalism, but in virtually every
instance his source of authority will be rationalism. This is
the prevailing base of authority in our day as a result of
modern science, of philosophical presuppositions, and of

some of the comparative studies in religion. Man has now come to the point where he feels that his own reason and his own experience must be the final criterion by which all is to be judged. The mind of modern man has become all important.

After filtering the Bible through the grid of his mind, William Newton Clarke drew an intellectual conclusion with reference to the New Testament writers' expectations of the imminent return of Jesus Christ. "I perceived that writers in the Bible had recorded unquestioning expectation of the almost immediate occurrence of an event that has never occurred at all. Certainly they were in error on that point. Their inspiration, of whatever kind it was, was not a safeguard against this error, but allowed them, or rather impelled them, to work their mistaken view of the immediate future into our holy book.... I was not required to accept all statements in the Bible as true and all views that it contained as correct."[1] This is a classic example of the working of rationalism in its attitude toward Scripture.

Historically, biblical Christianity has been based upon divine revelation, but today that position is being severely challenged. There was a time when the faithful, who were biblical theists, did not question the conviction that ultimate authority was Scripture. Whether they understood it or not, whether they agreed with it or not, whether they were able to penetrate into its meaning totally or not, it was nonetheless their final authority. However, for reasons which we will discuss in later chapters, that is now breaking down very remarkably and very quickly. We are seeing people who call themselves evangelicals operating from a different base of authority. This is crucial. Even though a person may deviate only slightly from the orthodox doctrines of the faith, if he has shifted to another base of authority he has nonetheless taken a very tragic step which may then lead him into further error. Even if he does not go on to further rejection of Scripture, he has opened the door for that possibility. Tragically, those to whom he ministers or those whom he teaches are likely to take his concepts to their logical conclusion.

At Six Flags Over Texas there used to be a great slide coming off the giant oil derrick. I can still recall the first time I went up on that thing with my children, who were quite young at the time. They were not allowed to go down by themselves because they were too small, but they could go down with an adult. I happened to be the adult. Sitting down on a burlap bag, with one child in front of me between my legs, I pushed myself over the edge and started down this frightening slope. As I did, I was tempted to reach out and grab the side. I found myself saying, *I don't really want to go down there this way. I am not sure just exactly how it will be when I go down there. I am not sure but that I might turn over or lose my grip on my son....* All kinds of terrible things went through my mind and imagination.

Many who have abandoned divine revelation as their final basis of authority, have, as it were, looked down at where they were going and, not liking what they saw, have reached out and grabbed the side; they are just hanging on. There is no logical reason why they should not just go on down. But, they simply do not want to go down. So there they hang, still fairly close to the top, but in a very unstable position.

There are people among us today, teaching in our institutions, laboring in our denomination, pastoring in our churches, who have not departed all that far from classic biblical doctrine. They still believe that Jesus is God. They still believe in the bodily resurrection of Christ. They still believe in the virgin birth. But, they do not believe that everything in Scripture is necessarily accurate and without error. They have started over the edge. They have abandoned divine revelation as their final basis of authority, however slight that deviation may seem to them. They do not want to slide all the way down to liberalism. They do not want to deny the faith outright. They do not want to reject all the basic doctrines of Christianity. As it were, they have simply grabbed hold of the side and stayed somewhere near the top. They profess most of the doctrines, but they claim there are some errors.

This stance may be almost imperceptible. There may not be a deliberate abandonment of a doctrinal position. They may not even know that they have headed downhill. But they are in an unstable position. Whether such individuals ever let go and slip further down or not, they are still in an unstable position. They are at least admitting the possibility of going further. It is also extremely likely that those to whom they minister or those whom they teach will go a lot farther down than they do.

This is illustrated abundantly in church history. In recent times, the death-of-God movement emerged as the ultimate conclusion of the teachings of some prominent theologians. They themselves did not take their theology that far. Those who were the leaders in the death-of-God movement, Altizer and Hamilton, were graduate students under Karl Barth and Paul Tillich. Both Tillich and Barth rejected the death-of-God hypothesis as being absurd, even heretical. Yet, Altizer and Hamilton said they were simply taking the thought of their teachers to its ultimate conclusion, which they reasoned to be the very death of God.

Every generation of students tends to take the teachings of its professors further than the professors themselves. If there is an opening, if there is a loophole, if there is some place to go with the teaching, they will go. Once we depart from divine revelation, we have at least opened the door to whatever deviation a person chooses to engage in. He may choose to deviate only slightly or he may choose to deviate in a tremendously dramatic way, but the choice is his. Once he has shifted from divine revelation to human reason as his basis of authority, he can go as far as he desires to go away from historic Christian conviction, and only his personal choice will determine where he stops. Thus, even those who have stopped relatively close to orthodoxy are still dangerous to the faith because they have opened the door to as much defection as anyone wants to engage in. Those who are coming after them will go further still. Ultimately, historic, biblical Christianity will be in shambles.

In this discussion of ultimate authority, the choice of terms is not the issue; the issue is the attitude toward the Scripture itself. It is important for me to affirm that it is not necessary for one to use the term *inerrancy.* It is also vital to say that not everyone who does not affirm the inerrancy of the Scriptures is a liberal, modernist or unbeliever. But the direction begun is a tragic step that could end in spiritual disaster.

We must reaffirm the great Reformation doctrine of *sola scriptura,* Scripture only, as being our final, ultimate base of authority and truth. Anything less than that is deficient and opens the door to every conceivable kind of theological distortion. But we are getting ahead of ourselves. Certain historical developments have had a dramatic effect on the people of God. We will look briefly at these in the next chapter.

CHAPTER 2

The Dramatic Shift Away from Biblical Authority

"The destructive critics have shifted from revelation to reason. The naturalistic uniformitarian scientists have shifted from revelation to reason. The philosophers have shifted from revelation to reason. The students of comparative religions have done the same. Authority becomes the result of the mind of man rather than the mind of God."

THE TERRIFYING TENDENCY of many in our day to take this tragic step has not come suddenly. It has been the subtle journey of many years. Prompted by a compromising position on the Word of God we have moved to a rationalistic base in many areas of the Christian community. How did this happen? How could people of such great confidence in the total reliability of the Scripture become people with such diluted convictions? It is important for us to trace the steps that have led to this compromising position.

The Historical-Critical Approach

This attitude has developed in four major areas. The first is in the emergence of the HISTORICAL-CRITICAL AP-PROACH TO SCRIPTURE, a difficult area to assimilate and understand. But we must try at least to grasp the essentials.

It would be helpful to distinguish between the various types of biblical criticism. The very term *critical* does not necessarily imply something negative. It simply refers to an intelligent, rational, research-oriented approach to Scripture. In itself, that is not bad. Only when it becomes destructive—rationalistic or naturalistic—is it objectionable.

We need to consider *textual criticism*. We do not have the original manuscripts of Scripture. Instead, we have many copies. It has been the task of textual criticism through the years to collate, compare, and sort through these many manuscripts, more than five thousand of them for the New Testament books alone, in order to try to restore the original text. Essentially, this has been done very satisfactorily, to the extent that we can say that the original text of Scripture has been substantially restored. It has been frequently pointed out by many scholars that no textual variation which we are currently wrestling with affects any basic doctrine of Christianity. Most of the textual variances are of a rather minor nature, having to do with relatively insignificant matters.

Secondly, we should discuss *linguistic criticism*. This has to do with the nature of the language, particularly of the New Testament. Until the late nineteenth century, many people felt that the Greek language of the New Testament was a very special, unique Greek used only in the New Testament. It was sometimes referred to as "Holy Ghost Greek." But with the discovery of numerous papyrus documents in Egypt it was determined that the Greek of the New Testament was the *koiné*, the common Greek used throughout the Mediterranean region in the first century. Thus, through the discovery of these letters, business documents, wills, and other writings, lexicographers were able to establish the meaning of words and the use of various idioms. This was a tremendous advance in our understanding of the New Testament language.

A third area of criticism is what we might call *literary criticism*. This area is sometimes divided into *lower criticism* and *higher criticism*, though the names are not particularly significant. They originally meant Step One and Step Two—the lower criticism had to be done before the higher criticism. Obviously, until we have a text to work with, we cannot do very much with it! Today, most critics are moving away from these terms, simply referring to this area as literary criticism. This does not deal with the integrity of the text, or the nature of the language; rather, it has to do with such things as authorship, date, occasion and place of writing, intended audience, and the basic integrity of the message itself. It also has to do with where the information came from, the form, and how it was put together by the author. Some subdivisions under literary criticism have become quite well known in the twentieth century.

The first of these, *source criticism,* has to do with the source of the material which the author used. For example, with regard to the Pentateuch, where did the information come from? What was the source? This, of course, has given rise to a great deal of speculation. About 1753, Jean Astruc, a French physician, noted the different names of God that appear in the Pentateuch. This gave rise to the theory that two different sources were evident there: one that knew *Jehovah* as the name of God, and the other that knew *Elohim* as the name of God. Shortly after that, J. G. Eichhorn took Astruc's work and combined with it his own analysis of the styles of the various sections of the Pentateuch to come up with a theory as to which portions came from one source and which came from another. This, of course, opened up a whole flood of inquiry; such men as Geddes (1792), Vater (ca. 1802), Ewald (ca. 1843), and Hupfeld (ca. 1853) made their contributions. As a result, when the works of these men were compiled, we have essentially what is known as the documentary hypothesis of the Pentateuch—the so-called JEDP theory. According to this theory, the five books of Moses were put together from four sources—two based upon the names of Jehovah and Elohim, plus a presumed Deuteronomic source and a presumed Priestly source. All of these, ostensibly, are to be seen in the composition of the Pentateuch.

In the New Testament, much the same thing has taken place. New Testament critics began to work on the Gospel accounts, particularly the synoptic Gospels—Matthew, Mark, and Luke—searching for the sources behind the Gospels. The popular view which finally emerged is that Mark was the original Gospel and that both Matthew and Luke drew from Mark as one of the primary sources for their own writings. Critics used the term "Q" (for the German word *quelle,* which means "source") for what they considered as another source, made up primarily of the sayings of Jesus. Presumably, Matthew and Luke drew some of their material from this source. So, we have Matthew and Luke drawing upon Mark and upon this "Q" source, plus, Matthew and Luke adding some material unique to themselves.

At this point, it should be noted that this type of procedure is not necessarily bad. It may well be that Mark was the original Gospel writer. I am inclined to think so myself. There may have been something like a "Q" source, although it probably consisted of a lot of oral information rather than being some document (which we have never found). Probably Matthew and Luke did add some material—Matthew, from his own eyewitness testimony, and Luke, from his own research.

But together with this source criticism there arose a basic skepticism about the reliability of the material. This is fundamental to our whole investigation. Such *destructive* literary criticism, seen particularly in source criticism and the others that we will consider presently, reevaluates the Bible as a purely human book. This whole process has sometimes been referred to as the historical-critical method.

George Ladd, in his *The New Testament and Criticism*, says, "The proponents of a thorough-going historical-critical method have insisted that historical study must be free from the restraint of any theological dogma, particularly from any doctrine of an inspired Scripture; that the biblical critic must be as open to any historical-critical conclusions as the researcher in the physical sciences must be open to the evidence of any and all facts; that any theological understanding of the Bible as the Word of God must automatically place a restraint and limitation upon the freedom of proper historical and critical investigation."[2]

Ladd goes on to say, however, that "the history of criticism shows that the proponents of a purely historical method themselves have not been motivated by a completely objective open-minded approach, but have approached the Bible with distinct philosophical and theological ideas about how it should be interpreted. In other words, their critical study was dominated by certain limiting presuppositions."[3]

What Ladd is saying, in effect, is that the historical-critical method of approaching the Scripture is basically a naturalistic, nonsupernaturalistic bias. Scripture is viewed as a purely human book and is, therefore, subject to all the foibles and problems involved with humanity. Since nobody is perfect, this view holds that no author of Scripture is perfect. Therefore, we are to look for flaws, we are to expect discrepancies, we are not surprised to find errors, we expect to find truth and untruth mixed together. In this process of study, the critical scholars say, we are to use all of the techniques of so-called scientific criticism, even as we would use them in the study of the works of Bacon, Spinoza, Shakespeare or Milton. Thus, at the very heart of the *destructive* historical-critical methodology is the fact that the Bible must be explained in totally naturalistic terms. That, of course, colors the whole process.

Form criticism is a little different, in that it seeks to determine the literary styles that are to be found in the text. For example, with regard to New Testament form criticism, the basic question that form critics have tried to answer is, "How did the historical Jesus become the Christ of faith?" This question is based upon the assumption that the Jesus who is pictured in the New Testament is not the real Jesus who actually lived. For the better part of the nineteenth century, critics were searching for the "historical Jesus," that is, they were attempting to go behind the actual words of the New Testament and discover the "real Jesus," the "simple carpenter," the "simple teacher." They were trying to find all of this underneath the complicated theology which, they say, somehow or other developed later and which was recorded in our New Testament. They attempted to separate the text into various literary units, such as narrative accounts, sayings, teachings, parables, and miracle stories. Each one of these, they believed, was somehow or other derived from the faith of the early church. In other words, what was found in the life of Jesus as recorded in the Gospels was not really what Jesus did and said so much as what the early church *remembered* about what Jesus did and said, and much of this was colored by tradition and by later teaching. Therefore, they concluded, we do not have real historical documents; we have the early church's theological faith remembrances of Jesus.

Then we have *redaction criticism.* A redactor is an editor. Therefore, redaction criticism has to do with how the writers may have put together their material. For example, whoever wrote the Gospel of Matthew was an editor, they say; he was not a historian. He was an editor and a theologian. Therefore, he picked and chose certain incidents out of the traditions of the early church concerning Jesus and put them together in a particular fashion so as to present a particular theological point of view. Redaction criticism attempts to determine what the writer was trying to prove. He was not just writing a history or a biography, according to this view. He was trying to prove something, and the way he put his material together will tell us what he was trying to prove.

Now, that is not altogether wrong. Obviously, the writers were trying to prove something. John said, "These are written that ye might believe that Jesus is the Christ, the Son of God" (John 20:31). But, again, it is the *negative* aspect of this approach that has become harmful. Most of the redaction critics have been rationalistic in their approach. Their thrust has not been to reproduce faithfully the theology of Christ or the theology of the New Covenant, but rather it has been to attempt a negative analysis of these writers who are perceived as putting together something which satisfied them, but which was not necessarily true historically and theologically.

The latest in the fads of criticism is *genre criticism,* from the French word *genre,* meaning kind or sort. Just as narrative, poetry, and biography are kinds of literature, so the *midrash* was a genre or kind of literature within the Semitic community. A midrash was a story that was used for teaching purposes. The whole point of genre criticism is to determine in each specific case what type of literature is being studied, what form it takes, what genre it is. If this can be done, we can then proceed to interpret the particular piece of literature correctly. When we ask what sort of methodology a writer has used to tell his parable or write his apocalyptic story, and how it is to be understood, and what are the principles for interpreting it, we are engaged in *genre criticism*.

When applied to the Gospels, for example, genre criticism makes the author not only a redactor, or editor, dealing with sources, but also an innovator, an originator of material. For instance, Matthew, according to these critics, was trying to present a particular theological point of view. In so doing, he put together a lot of material from the traditions concerning Jesus and His disciples. But because the material itself was not sufficient for his purposes, he made up some material himself. In other words, the Gospels are said to be of the genre midrash, in which the rabbis used to create material in order to present a point. According to this point of view, Matthew (and, presumably, Luke and Mark) made up some events and sayings and presented them in historical form to provide the framework for the message that he was trying to present.

According to the genre critic, those who did this were not being deceitful, they were not lying, they were not trying to present something under false pretenses. They were just using an established type of literature to get a point across. If we understood the type of literature they were writing, we would not be offended by the fact that they did it in this way. Furthermore, if we understood the type of literature they were writing, we could interpret it correctly. This would relieve us of the mistaken necessity of trying to take everything in the Gospel literally, as though Jesus actually said a thing verbatim, actually did this or that, went there, saw this, and spoke these words.

Genre criticism, again, has its place, but in a very limited realm. If we can understand the type of literature that the man is writing, obviously it will help us to interpret that literature. But when we start saying that the biblical writer made up events that never occurred and created sayings which Jesus and the apostles never uttered, then the critic has gone far beyond the legitimate limits of criticism into destructive criticism, once again doing violence to the integrity of the text.

We can trace this *destructive* literary criticism back a long way. For example, the Jewish philosopher Benedict Spinoza, who lived in the seventeenth century, was a forerunner of modern higher criticism. If we browse through his writings, we will note that he points out that the Bible contains contradictions. This did not bother him. He maintained that the Bible does not contain propositional revelation, that is, actual statements of fact. As a matter of fact, he said that those who hold to such a view have set the Bible above God. Spinoza, like Bacon and Hobbes before him, taught that the authority of the Bible was purely in religious matters. He did not think that the Bible had anything to say about secular matters, and, therefore, we should not look to the Bible for answers in matters of science and history—only in matters of faith and morals. Spinoza also denied the miraculous in Scripture.

We also note the philosophy of Hegel (1770-1831), best known as a dialectic. He reasoned that there is a tension between one position, the *thesis,* and a second position, the *antithesis.* As these two interact, eventually a *synthesis* (a third position) emerges, bringing into light a new aspect of reality. Then, this synthesis becomes the thesis all over again, and an opposing position, another antithesis, comes into play, resulting in a new synthesis, and on and on—sort of an evolutionary development of thought.

In the nineteenth century, F. C. Baur, who was a professor at Tübingen in Germany, applied this Hegelian philosophy to the New Testament. Briefly, his reasoning went like this: there are two contradictory strands of teaching in the New Testament. One can be identified with the Apostle

Paul. His is the theology of grace, the theology of salvation by faith alone. The other is the theology essentially of Simon Peter and the Jerusalem church. This is the legalistic philosophy or theology reflected in James, teaching a salvation based upon law-keeping and legalism. Ultimately, these two points of view, the thesis and the antithesis, came together into a synthesis, and that synthesis is what we finally have in the New Testament, although we can see strands of both throughout.

Baur thought that Paul wrote only four epistles. He accepted Romans, 1 and 2 Corinthians, and Galatians as being authentically Pauline. The rest he felt were not in keeping with his hypothesis; therefore, he made the facts fit his hypothesis. Although that particular viewpoint is not as popular as it was a hundred years ago, it still can be seen in the thinking of many rationalistic theologians today. So we have still another philosophical strand that has affected biblical criticism.

What we see essentially is that during the seventeenth century and, with a vengeance in the eighteenth century, there developed a viewpoint that Scripture is a human book written by human beings, with the same hangups, the same foibles, the same fallible, inherent capabilities that all men have. Therefore, we must treat Scripture as any other book. We must apply to it all of the methods of historical criticism as we would any other book.

These techniques are not totally without value. But when in the hands of a naturalist, a skeptic who does not accept the supernatural element in Scripture, they become very destructive and ultimately deny the very essence of biblical Christianity. This has been one of the major thrusts against basic, biblical Christianity in the last two hundred years and more. The historical-critical method offers some good tools for Bible students, but it makes a terrible master.

Dr. Benjamin C. Fisher, former head of the Southern Baptist Education Commission, recently said, ". . . the application of scientific and linguistic analysis to the evaluation and interpretation of biblical literature brought about profound changes in our view of the historical Jesus and the trustworthiness of the Scriptures. For many people this raised serious questions as to whether the Scriptures are a gift from God or, especially in the case of the resurrection of Jesus, a wish-fulfillment of the early Christian community."[4]

Existential Philosophy

The second major factor contributing to the shift away from biblical authority is the rise of EXISTENTIAL PHILOSOPHY and its application to theology. In classical philosophy, two views have prevailed with regard to how one knows truth. One is the rationalistic view, which says that there is something intuitive and basic in man's mind which enables him to determine truth by reasoning alone. The other is empiricism, which says that man knows truth by his senses. Immanuel Kant, regarded by many as perhaps the most important philosopher of all time, tried to reconcile these two aspects. In his classic work, *The Critique of Pure Reason,* Kant sought to combine rationalism and empiricism into a new epistemological system. His concept—summarized briefly and slightly oversimplified—was this: both the rationalist and empiricist are right, but both are wrong, up to a certain point. It is true, he says, that we gain our knowledge from experience, from empirical sources. But, he says, the mind possesses basic intuitive abilities by which man arranges and catalogs the sense information which comes into the mind. So, both faculties are involved—the basic abilities, the filing system as it were, furnished by the mind, and the data which comes into the mind through empirical sensation.

More important, from our standpoint, Kant concluded that no knowledge of God is possible through scientific methodology because God is above empirical investigation. Since we have no intuitive knowledge of God, the existence and reality of God must be established on some basis other than rationalism or empiricism. What was that basis? Essentially, he said (and this he carried further in two of his later works, *The Critique of Practical Reason* and *Religion within the Limits of Reason Alone*) that although religion cannot be sustained by reason or by empirical investigation, it is nonetheless valuable in our lives because of moral necessity. In other words, we need religion in order to live moral lives and to have a reasonably moral and stable society, even though it is not possible to establish its validity, either by empiricism or rationalism.

I do not think that Kant had any desire to destroy Christianity. He, in effect, wanted to place it beyond the reach of philosophical and scientific investigation and thus, hopefully, safe from both. But the result was quite different. His readers and hearers took him to mean that since religion cannot be substantiated either by empirical investigation or by intuitive reasoning, then God probably does not even really exist. Probably there is no God and probably religion is not valid. Kant tried to salvage this by his moral argument, but was not altogether successful.

The German theologian, Friedrich Schleiermacher (1768–1834), was a professor of theology at the University of Berlin. About 1800, he took Kant's philosophy and tried to bring a theology out of it. In essence, he concluded that it was true that as a result of the philosophical work of Kant and the findings of the biblical critics, there probably was no way to establish the validity of Christianity. He felt it could not be established from the standpoint of an authoritative Bible, from man's own reason or from his empirical investigation. Nonetheless, he said, we must retain Christianity because it is necessary for our experience. The essence of his position was, "Let's try to retain the experience of Christianity, even though we do not have the empirical or revelational basis for it that we once thought we had."

This is where the so-called "two-story" concept comes in. Think of a two-story building. The first floor is biblical authority and revelation. The second story is Christian experience. Historically, the second floor had always been built on the first one; Christian experience had always grown out of biblical revelation and biblical authority. But now, philosophically and critically, the first floor has in effect been destroyed; Schleiermacher was willing to concede this. But he was not willing to concede the demise of the second floor. So we have, in effect, the second floor suspended in space as by a theological skyhook.

This particular philosophy—experience without a firm basis of biblical authority—is where much of contemporary theology finds itself. It is seen very graphically in modern neoorthodoxy. Neoorthodox theologians still talk about Jesus, salvation, and faith, yet they believe that the Bible is absolutely shot through with contradictions, errors, primitive cosmologies, and pagan concepts. This is essentially what we mean by existential theology. Existential theology is a theology based on human experience rather than upon any divine revelation or divine authority. Essentially, it means that we can have the experience of God without a propositional revelation from God.

There are degrees of existential theology. There is the left wing, which might be reflected in Rudolf Bultmann. The "middle" wing might be reflected in Karl Barth and Emil Brunner. Then there is the right wing, which includes some

people today who call themselves evangelicals. There are
Southern Baptists today who will tell us that they believe in
Jesus, that they believe in the resurrection, that they believe
in salvation through faith; but they do not believe in a completely authoritative Bible, and they do not see any necessity
for such a Bible. Why? Because God, in some existential,
mystical way, can speak to them through a Bible which in
itself is not necessarily accurate in every respect. They do
not care whether the Bible is altogether accurate or not. It is
of no concern to them. All they are concerned about is their
religious experience based upon an "encounter" with God
through the Bible—and even through the imperfections of
the Bible.

Karl Barth went so far as to say that God intentionally
allowed imperfections in the Scripture so as to cause an even
greater trust on the part of His people who could have faith
in spite of all the imperfections. This is the ultimate in philosophical absurdity!

Where is the danger? Is it not true that we want to have a
personal experience with God? Is it not true that putting it
all into practice and having a genuine experience with God
is more important than the minutiae and details? But that is
not the point. The point is that all of it thus becomes *subjec-
tive.* It all becomes *mystical and existential.* When we begin
to deny the historical, scientific, geographical, and chronological accuracy of Scripture, what logical reason do we
have for retaining the "theological facts"? If it does not
make any difference how accurate the Bible is, if just what
God says to us through the Bible is essential, then how do
we know that what He says about the atonement is necessarily factual? How do we know that what He says about the
resurrection is necessarily true? Eventually, the central core
of Christian faith is replaced with some sort of a vapid, self-
centered experience. That is the great danger when sub-

jectivism and mysticism replace actual propositional revelation.

Naturalistic, Uniformitarian Science

The third challenge to basic biblical Christianity is the rise of NATURALISTIC, UNIFORMITARIAN SCIENCE. Uniformitarianism, essentially, means that the universe operates now as it has always operated. There are universal principles that have always been in operation. There has been no intervention or interruption by anything or anyone supernatural.

This development in virtually every field of science took place concurrently with the growing acceptance of the historical-critical method in biblical studies and the evolution in philosophy that I have just described. The early champions of naturalistic, uniformitarian science were James Hutton and Charles Lyell. In 1830, Lyell set forth in his *Principles of Geology* an explanation of geology which did not depend upon any supernatural element. Everything in geology could be explained totally on the basis of natural causes without supernatural intervention. Charles Darwin in 1859 in his *Origin of Species,* and in 1871 in his *Descent of Man,* picked up that same basic uniformitarian thinking and applied it to the study of biology.

This same uniformitarianism has been applied in the social sciences as well—Sigmund Freud, for example, in the area of psychology, and Emile Durkheim in sociology. Freud believed that "God" is simply an extension of man's needs. Man grew up with a human father and he depended upon him to meet most of his needs. When it was no longer possible for his human father to meet his needs, he created a cosmic father. So, God, according to Freud, is simply that which is created by man because of a psychological need.

Durkheim and others in the area of sociology said that "God" was simply a figment of man's imagination, intended to explain that which is unexplainable, and to placate that which they feared. What man could not control—such as fire, wind, flood, the sun and moon—he tended to worship and sought to appease. When everything is viewed from a naturalistic standpoint, God and the Bible are essentially eliminated. This has given rise to the whole evolutionary theory which is so prominent in our day and has done away with any concept of divine creationism or of man as being created in the image of God. This obviously has had tremendous effect upon biblical Christianity, presumably discrediting significant portions of Scripture entirely because they do not agree with this uniformitarian, naturalistic, skeptical, essentially atheistic, position.

Presumed Contributions of Comparative Religions

The fourth major factor is the STUDY OF COMPARATIVE RELIGIONS AND THEIR PRESUMED CONTRIBUTIONS TO CHRISTIANITY. The basic idea here is that unbelieving scholars, in their study of the other religions and traditions of men, have found similarities between these religions and the Judeo-Christian beliefs. They have concluded that religion has evolved on the earth just like everything else and that man's concept of deity is evolving and emerging; starting all the way back at the beginning with primitive animism and polytheism, over many, many generations, monotheism has finally developed. Christianity is now, presumably, the highest form of monotheism, they say. Nonetheless, Christianity has been shaped by all of the other religions of man and thus is not to be considered unique; it is simply a more refined and developed view of God, morality, and ethics.

Let me give two or three examples. There is an ancient account of Creation from the Babylonian tradition which is called the Enuma Elish. It probably dates several hundred years earlier than Genesis, yet there are some remarkable similarities. In both accounts, the earth, following Creation, is said to be empty and void. There follows, in the Babylonian account, an essentially similar order of events, from a watery chaos to the eventual "rest" of the deity. The number seven is prominent—the seven days of Creation in Genesis are matched by the seven cantos or tablets in the Enuma Elish. Yet, there are striking differences. For instance, the Genesis account presupposes monotheism, whereas the Babylonian account presupposes a gross polytheism.

A second example is the Babylonian flood account, the Epic of Gilgamesh. Again, it is very similar to the Genesis flood account, and was probably written at least two hundred years earlier than Genesis. The great flood is planned by the gods. The impending catastrophe is revealed to the hero. In the Gilgamesh story, the hero is Utnapishtim; in the biblical account, it is Noah. In both accounts, the flood is connected with the defection of the human race. In both, the hero and his family are delivered by means of a huge boat and special blessings are conferred on the hero after the flood subsides. But again, there are striking differences. We have monotheism in the Genesis account, polytheism in the Gilgamesh story. Genesis is on a high moral plane, while immorality, even among the gods, characterizes the Babylonian account.

How do we explain this? Here are Babylonian accounts of Creation and the Flood which admittedly predate Genesis by at least two centuries. The rationalistic critic says that there is only one way to explain this—admit that the Genesis account was drawn from the Babylonian story and was changed somewhat to make it more compatible with the religion of Israel. Thus, we must not look upon the Jewish Scriptures as being particularly unique. They are simply adaptations from the writings of other cultures and religions which were synthesized, modified, and added to until the formation of what we call the Old Testament.

Here is a New Testament example: the Golden Rule. "In everything, do to others what you would have them do to you. . . ." (Matthew 7:12 NIV), which Jesus taught in the Sermon on the Mount. The critics point out to us that Hinduism has a Golden Rule, Buddhism has a Golden Rule. Likewise, Zoroastrianism, Confucianism, Taoism, Greek philosophy—all have a Golden Rule. All of these predate the enunciation of the Golden Rule by Jesus, so what is so unique?

What about the miraculous birth and the miraculous preexistence of Jesus? Critics say there is nothing so unusual about these either. Gautama the Buddha is said, in Buddhist literature, to have had a miraculous birth. The same is claimed for Lao-tze, founder of Taoism. So also Mahavira of Jainism and Zoroaster of Zoroastrianism. All of these, along with Jesus, are said to have had a supernatural origin and were in some way related to the gods.

Rudolf Bultmann made a great deal of the so-called "Gnostic redeemer myth." Here was folklore in the first century, he says, that was very similar to the biblical accounts and was ultimately picked up by the Christian writers.

All of this, they say, is proof that Christianity is not unique, that Jesus is not unique, that it is all a product of the cultures, the traditions, and the civilizations which went before and which existed simultaneously with Judaism and Christianity. This has had a profound effect upon how biblical Christianity is regarded today, and it has driven many away from traditional biblical theology.

We need to point out essentially how these similarities are to be accounted for, though we cannot do that in great detail here. Concerning the Creation and Flood accounts, there are two ways of understanding the phenomena. It is theoretically possible, from a naturalistic standpoint, that the Genesis accounts are derived from the Babylonian stories. That, however, does not make a great deal of sense, even from a purely scholarly point of view, because a derivation is normally less than the original, not more; less simple, less noble, less inspiring than the original, not greater. It is not very likely that one would take an account and raise it to the majesty of Genesis by drawing from the rather dreary, polytheistic, immoral narratives of the Babylonians. It is much more likely that the biblical explanation is the right one—that there really was a divine creation and a flood, and that when Moses recorded what we now have in Genesis, he wrote down something that actually occurred and he wrote it by divine inspiration. If the Creation and the Flood really took place, we would expect memories of these to filter down through all peoples and all civilizations, including the ancient Babylonians. Therefore, it is not surprising that they have in their tradition stories of a creation and a flood, because those things actually happened and the stories were passed down orally from generation to generation. But not being preserved by divine revelation, they became garbled.

When we come to such things as the origin of the founders of the world religions, it is true that there is a Buddhist tradition that Gautama, who lived hundreds of years before Jesus, was also miraculously born. But if we will check it out very carefully, we will find that the particular Buddhist writings which record this were not written until after Jesus was born. The same thing is true of Lao-tze, Confucius, Zoroaster, and Mahavira. Although some of these people lived long before Jesus did, the commentaries which bring their stories into approximate conformity with the Christian story were not written until after Jesus. So, hundreds of years after Gautama lived, some of his Buddhist followers began to read back into his story some of the facts which were picked up and borrowed from Christianity. In other words, it is just the opposite of what the rationalists are saying. It is not that Christianity borrowed from these religions; these religions borrowed from Christianity.

Concerning the Golden Rule, this was undoubtedly a part of God's original revelation to the human race, preserved in varying forms by differing peoples. Once again, it all depends on one's presupposition. If we begin with the idea that there was no Creation, that there is no God, that there is no such thing as the supernatural, that there is no divine revelation, then we are forced to some conclusions simply because there seems to be no other alternative. But if we start with the biblical framework of a Creator God and a Revealer God, then all of these things begin to fit together into a very different explanation. This skepticism over the last one hundred and fifty years has been very destructive to biblical Christianity.

These areas of concern represent a significant, but mostly overlooked shift from divine revelation to rationalism as the ultimate base of authority. The destructive critics have shifted from revelation to reason. The naturalistic, uniformitarian scientists have shifted from revelation to reason. The philosophers have shifted from revelation to reason. The students of comparative religions, likewise. Ultimately, all of these attacks have come because of the shift in the base of authority from revelation to reason.

This has led, first of all, to religious experience without theological foundation—the two-story effect we mentioned earlier. We now have around us in rationalistic circles, in neoorthodox circles, and in quasi-evangelical circles (which are really still neoorthodox) the idea that religious experience can survive .without an authoritative revelation from God in Scripture. IT CANNOT ULTIMATELY SURVIVE! But there are those who are trying to place it on that basis. The great emphasis is on experience as being the measure of truth: if I have had a real experience that "blesses" me, they say, then it must be right regardless of what the Scripture says. Such theology leads away from God, not toward God.

This has also led to relativistic ethics, so-called "situational ethics." If there is no propositional revelation from God, if there are no direct commands from God, then, obviously, there are no moral absolutes. This has led to the whole gamut of aberrations in the area of ethics. We might point out here that if there is no authority from God, if there are no moral absolutes, then we have no certainty about anything. The secular humanists are saying that society can exist successfully without any word from a deity, or as one writer has said, "without benefit of clergy." But it cannot ultimately exist successfully.

How do we know that we ought to restrain murder? Or that murder is wrong? Or that rape is wrong? Or that armed robbery is wrong? Or that embezzlement is wrong? Well, someone says, everyone knows that these are wrong. No, everyone does not know they are wrong. There are many people in our prisons who apparently did not know they are wrong. If we do not have any moral absolutes, then we cannot establish that something is wrong. They say we establish it by common consensus. But suppose the consensus changes, as it apparently did in Nazi Germany when it was considered proper to perpetrate the tragic massacre of the holocaust. All of this results from a lack of moral absolutes.

Then, finally (and this is very important with regard to our Southern Baptist Convention), all of this leads to a so-called evangelism without any biblical concept of man's actual condition or God's revealed response. Even the rationalists and the neoorthodox talk about evangelism. But they are not talking about the same thing that biblical Christians are talking about. They do not have any basis for biblical evangelism. They do not think that man is actually lost, or that there is a hell or eternal punishment. They do not think there is need for or reality in a substitutionary atonement. Many of them do not believe there was a bodily resurrection of Jesus Christ. Therefore, to them, evangelism becomes quite a different thing.

We need to be cautious that while we are talking of going on with evangelism and missions, those with whom we are speaking have the same thing in mind that we do. Other denominations, once great for God, are talking about evangelism and missions, but they mean something quite different. And they show the effects of this devastating shift away from biblical authority which, as we have seen, is a contradiction of biblical Christianity. Without an authoritative divine revelation, worship degenerates into mere form and ritual, ministry concerns itself only with the temporal and the physical, and authority becomes the result of the mind of man rather than the mind of God.

It is vitally important for us to examine the positions taken on the authority of the Bible by the early church fathers and by our Baptist forebears. We will turn our attention to these two historical areas now, taking note of how their views on authority impacted on the church's witness and missionary effectiveness.

CHAPTER 3

The Church's Historical Position on Biblical Authority

"Look carefully into the Scriptures which are the true utterances of the Holy Spirit."

Clement of Rome, ca. A.D. 100

THERE IS MUCH discussion today about the historical belief and practice of the church regarding the nature of Scripture. It is routine for those who believe in the full authority of Scripture—that is, biblical inerrancy—to be characterized as ultraconservatives, as bibliolaters (those who worship the Bible rather than God), as those who make the Bible a paper pope. It is claimed that the doctrine of biblical inerrancy is a recent development, that it derives from post-Reformation scholasticism and that it does not have its roots in the church fathers and in the mainstream of Christian theology.

A recent book by Jack Rogers and Donald McKim, *The Authority and Interpretation of the Bible: An Historical Approach,* attempts to document this particular position. The authors claim that modern-day fundamentalists have departed from the historic understanding of the church with regard to the nature of Scripture and as a result have caused confusion and division within the body of Christ today. (For a complete and scholarly refutation of this position, refer to the subsequent work by John Woodbridge, *Biblical Authority*). It is our purpose in this chapter to demonstrate rather briefly that the Christian church down through the centuries has believed in the full authority of Scripture and that modern-day evangelicals who continue to support this view of Scripture are in the mainstream of Christian orthodoxy. Actually, those who have departed from this position are the ones who have introduced novelty into the Christian church and who are causing division within the body of Christ.

One of the earliest of the church fathers, outside of the apostles themselves, to write anything which has been preserved for us today was Clement of Rome who died in A.D. 102. Clement said, ". . . look carefully into the Scriptures which are the true utterances of the Holy Spirit." Even from this very brief quotation, there can be no doubt that Clement understood the Scriptures to be inspired by the Holy Spirit of God and thus to be absolutely reliable.

Justin Martyr (ca. 105-165), one of the most famous of the early Christian apologists, said, ". . . that we must not suppose that the language proceeds from the men who are inspired but from the divine word which moves them." Justin also said, ". . . the history which Moses wrote by divine inspiration . . . the Holy Spirit of prophecy taught through him." Surely there can be no doubt concerning Justin's position with regard to the full inspiration of Scripture or of the Mosaic authorship of the Pentateuch.

Irenaeus, bishop of Gaul in the late second century A.D., was also unambiguous in his statements concerning Scripture. "All Scripture as it has been given to us by God will be found to be harmonious." Again, he said, ". . . the Scriptures are perfect, inasmuch as they were uttered by the word of God and His Spirit, though we want the knowledge of their mysteries." Again, Irenaeus, although admitting that we are not always capable of interpreting Scripture perfectly, nonetheless clearly states his belief in the perfection of Scripture as originally written.

Clement of Alexandria (A.D. 150-217) said this about Scripture: "There is no discord between the law and the gospel, but harmony for they both proceed from the same author." Again, Clement said, ". . . of which [the Scriptures] not one tittle shall pass away without being accomplished for the mouth of the Lord, the Holy Spirit, spoke it." Clement, too, expresses his complete confidence in the divine origin of Scripture and its complete accuracy.

Clement's colleague, Origen (A.D. 185-253), also of Alexandria, was clearly unambiguous in his view of Scripture. "We cannot say of the writings of the Holy Spirit, that anything in them is useless or superfluous, even if they seem to some obscure." In another place Origen said that the Scriptures "breathe the spirit of fullness and there is nothing whether in the law or in the prophets, in the evangelists or the apostles which does not descend from the fullness of the divine majesty." Again, Origen said, ". . . believing that the divine foreknowledge which supplies superhuman wisdom to the race of man by the Scriptures, has placed, so to speak, the seeds of saving truth in each letter. . . ."

The opponents of biblical inerrancy in the twentieth century have tended to ridicule the so-called "domino theory," that is, that if any error at all can be found in Scripture, the credibility of all Scripture will be damaged. It is interesting to note that this theory did not originate with the twentieth century. Consider this quote by the church father, Cyprian (died A.D. 258): ". . . the gospel cannot stand in part and fall in part. . . ." We will see that he was not the only church father who expressed concern in this area.

Athanasius (died A.D. 373), the great defender of Christian orthodoxy at the Council of Nicea in A.D. 325, said, "In the words of the Scripture is the Lord." A reading of his contest with Arius at the Council of Nicea will demonstrate that h~ used the full authority of Scripture effectively in his argument concerning the full deity of Jesus Christ.

Augustine (A.D. 354-430), considered by many to be the greatest theologian of the ancient church, was also quite clear in expressing his views concerning the integrity of Scripture. "Only to those books which are called canonical have I learned to give honor so that I believe most firmly that no author in these books made any error in writing. . . . I read other authors, not with the thought that what they have taught and written is true, just because they have manifested holiness and learning." Note that Augustine explicitly states that no author of any biblical book made any error in writing. How does this differ from the modern definition of biblical inerrancy? The answer is that it does not differ in any sense whatsoever. On another occasion, Augustine said, "Therefore, we yield to and agree to the authority of the Holy Scripture which can neither be deceived nor deceive."

Jerome (A.D. 342-420), also one of the great scholars of the early church, is perhaps most famous as the translator of the Latin Vulgate edition of the Bible. Jerome stated, "When you are really instructed in the divine Scriptures and have realized that its laws and testimonies are the bonds of truth, then you can contend with adversaries, then you will fetter them and lead them bound into captivity, then of the foes you have made captive, you will make free men of God." Obviously, Jerome believed the Scriptures to be absolutely authoritative and thus valuable in their use against the enemies of Christianity.

Thomas Aquinas (A.D. 1225-1274), is considered by most Christians to have been the most influential theologian of the Middle Ages. What was his view of Scripture? Consider the following section from his writing:

However, sacred doctrine makes use of these authorities [philosophers] only as extraneous and probable arguments. Properly, theology uses the authorities of the canonical Scripture as the necessary argumentation. The authority of the doctors of the church is properly employed but as merely probable, for our faith rests upon the revelation given to the apostles and prophets who wrote the canonical books and not on revelation (if there be such a thing) made to other teachers. Whence, Augustine said in his letter to Jerome, "Only to those books which are called canonical have I learned to give honor so that I believe most firmly that no author in any of these books made any error in writing. I read other authors, not with the thought that what they have taught and written is true just because they have manifested holiness and learning."

Note that Thomas Aquinas agreed precisely with the position of Augustine whom we quoted earlier. Representing as he does the theological attitude of the medieval church, does not his writing demonstrate that the church in that era held to the full authority and inspiration of Holy Scripture as did the early church?

Let us move on to the time of the Protestant Reformation. Martin Luther (A.D. 1483-1546) was absolutely clear and precise concerning his view of biblical inspiration despite the attempts of many today to muddy the waters concerning Luther's theology. Consider some of his prominent statements. "This is our foundation where the Holy Scripture establishes something that must be believed, there we must not deviate from the words as they sound, neither from the order as it stands unless an express article of faith (based on clear Scripture passages) compels us to interpret the words otherwise, or arrange them differently. Else, what would become of the Bible?"

The following quote indicates that Luther also held to a "domino theory." "They do not believe that they [the words of Scripture] are God's words. For if they believed they were God's words, they would not call them poor, miserable words but would regard such words and titles as greater than the whole world and would fear and tremble before them as before God Himself. For whoever despises a single word of God does not regard any as important." Or consider the following statement from Luther: "Whoever is so bold that he ventures to accuse God of fraud and deception in a single word and does so willfully again and again after he has been warned and instructed once or twice will likewise certainly venture to accuse God of fraud and deception in all of His words. Therefore, it is true, absolutely and without deception that everything is believed or nothing is believed. The Holy Spirit does not suffer Himself to be separated or divided so that He should teach and cause to be believed one doctrine rightly and another falsely."

Certainly, Luther was a man of plain speech and it is difficult indeed to misinterpret the precise thought which he expresses in these words, that is, that Scripture is the Word of God and if one rejects any of it, he is, in effect, rejecting all of it. This is the essence of Protestant, Reformation theology.

John Calvin (A.D. 1509-1564), the father of Presbyterian and Reformed theology, is likewise unambiguous in his statements concerning Scripture. At varying places in his writings, he refers to Scripture as "the sure and infallible record," "the inerring standard," "the pure word of God," "the infallible rule of His holy truth," "free from every stain or defect," "the inerring certainty," "the certain and unerring rule," "the infallible word of God," "inviolable," "infallible oracles." These are hardly the statements of a man who believed that the Scriptures contained error.

Consider also what is generally thought to be Calvin's classic statement on Scripture:

> When it pleased God to raise up a more visible form of the church, He willed to have His word set down and sealed in writing. . . . He commanded also that the prophecies be committed to writing and be accounted part of His word. To these, at the same time, histories were added, also the labor of the prophets but composed under the Holy Spirit's dictation. I include the Psalms with the Prophecies. . . . That whole body, therefore, made up of law, prophecies, psalms and histories was the Lord's Word for the ancient people.
>
> Let this be a firm principle, no other word is to be held as the Word of God, and given place as such in the Church, than what is contained first in the Law and the Prophets, then in the writings of the apostles. . . . [the apostles] were to expound the ancient Scripture and to show that what is taught there has been fulfilled in Christ. Yet, they were not to do this except from the Lord, that is, with Christ's Spirit going before them and in a sense dictating their words. . . . [They] were sure and genuine penmen of the Holy Spirit and their writings are therefore to be considered oracles of God and the sole office of others is to teach what is provided and sealed in the Holy Scriptures.

Calvin also said:

> In order to uphold the authority of Scripture, he [Paul] declares it to be divinely inspired. For if it

be so, it is beyond all controversy that men should
receive it with reverence. . . . Whoever, then,
wishes to profit in the Scriptures, let him first of all
lay down as a settled point this—that the law and
the prophecies are not teachings delivered by the
will of men, but dictated by the Holy Ghost. . . .
Moses and the prophets did not utter at random
what we have from their hand, but since they
spoke by divine impulse, they confidently and
fearlessly testified, as was actually the case, that it
was the mouth of the Lord that spoke. . . . We owe
to the Scripture the same reverence which we owe
to God, because it has proceeded from Him
alone. . . .

Can there be any question whatsoever concerning John
Calvin's commitment to total biblical authority and inerrancy? Absolutely not!

One of the most influential preachers and theologians of
the early American scene was Jonathan Edwards (A.D.
1703-1758). Along with George Whitefield, Edwards was a
leader in the Great Awakening of the eighteenth century
which shaped to no small degree the early political and cul-
tural development of our nation. His view of Scripture can
be seen in the following statement:

The Scriptures are evidence of their own divine
authority as a human being is evident by the mo-
tions, behavior and speech of a body of a human
form and contexture, or, that the body is animated
by a rational mind. For we know no otherwise
than by the consistency, harmony and concurrence
of the train of actions and sounds, and their agreement to all that we can suppose to be a rational

mind. . . . So there is that wondrous universal harmony and consent and concurrence in the aim and drift such as universal appearance of a wonderful, glorious design, such stamps everywhere of exalted and divine wisdom, majesty, and holiness in matter, manner, contexture and aim, that the evidence is the same that the Scriptures are the word and work of a divine mind; to one that is thoroughly acquainted with them, as 'tis that the words and actions of an understanding man are from a rational mind, to one that is of a long time been his familiar acquaintance.

These selected quotations from some of the most prominent and influential of the church fathers indicate beyond any doubt that a belief in the full integrity and accuracy of Scripture has been an integral part of the church's belief from the very earliest times. Now we turn our attention to our own particular heritage as Baptists, to see what a brief review of Baptist history has to teach us concerning our historic position on the doctrine of Scripture.

CHAPTER 4

Baptists' Historical Position on Biblical Authority

"Did the inspired writers receive everything by direct revelation? The inspired writers learned many things by observation or inquiry, but they were preserved by the Holy Spirit from error; whether in learning or in writing these things."

John Broadus

ALTHOUGH HISTORIANS are not unanimous concerning the origin of the people whom we today know as Baptists, most Baptist historians would probably agree that the roots of our modern Baptist movement are to be found in the sixteenth- and seventeenth-century Protestant Reformation. Many Christians who were dissatisfied with the Roman Catholic system began a movement of purification from any trace of Roman Catholic tradition. These people became known as Puritans. For a time they remained in the Church of England, but later they became disillusioned and decided to form their own assemblies. As such, they became known as Separatists and eventually as Baptists because of their firm belief in believer's baptism for adults.

Most Baptist historians would identify the first Baptist church to be the one established in Amsterdam in 1609. The leader of that church was John Smyth, a highly educated man with both bachelor's and master's degrees from Cambridge University. What was Smyth's view of Scripture? He leaves no doubt in our minds as this quotation from *Baptists and the Bible* shows:

> Men are of two sortes, Inspired or ordinary men. Men Inspired by the Holy Ghost are the Holy Prophets and Apostles who wrote the holy scriptures by inspiration. 2 Peter 1.21, 2 Tim. 3.16, Rom. 1.2, namely the Hebrue of the ould testament and the greeke of the New Testament. The holy scriptures viz. the originalls Hebrew and Greek are given by Divine Inspiration and in their first donation were without error, most perfect and therefore Canonicall.

It is extremely instructive to note that not only did Smyth believe in the full inspiration of Scripture, but that he clearly distinguished between the original manuscripts of Scripture and the copies and translations which came later. Many are telling us today that there is no precedent for distinguishing between the original manuscripts and the editions which we have today. Notice, however, that one of the first Baptists clearly made that distinction, and that distinction has been observed and recognized down through the generations since his time, as we shall see.

At about the same time John Smyth was leading the church at Amsterdam, another early Baptist, Thomas Helwys, was authoring a confession of faith (1611) entitled *A Declaration of Faith of English People Remaining at Amsterdam in Holland.* Most Baptist historians regard this as the first English Baptist confession of faith. Notice the doctrine of Scripture contained in that confession:

That the Scriptures off the Old and New Testament are written for our instruction, 2 Tim. 3.16
and that we ought to search them for they testifie
of Christ, Jo. 5.39. And therefore to bee used with
all reverence, as conteyning the Holie Word off
God, which onclie is our direction in all things
whatsoever.

Note that Helwys was seemingly unaware of the modern
distinction between the so-called "theological" content of
Scripture and the so-called "secular" content of Scripture.
He said that Scripture "is our direction in all things whatsoever." Presumably, this would mean science, history, chronology, and geography as well as theology.

Another prominent seventeenth-century Baptist cler-
gyman was Thomas Grantham (1634-1692). His view of
Scripture is clearly set forth in this quotation:

We therefore conclude that such hath been the
Providence of God, that Men could not corrupt
those Holy Writings which he had ordained for the
Generations to come; neither can all the Art of
Evil Men rase out, or foist into the Greek copies,
so much as one Sentence, but either Friend or Foe
would soon detect them.

It should be obvious that Grantham agreed with Helwys
and Smyth concerning the inspiration of Scripture.

The Second London Confession (1688-1689) is one of the
more influential Baptist statements of faith. It is the Baptist
revision of the famous Westminster Confession which became the founding theological document of the Presbyterian
and Reformed churches. The statement on Holy Scripture is
very extensive but two brief excerpts will capture the flavor

of the statement. "The Authority of the Holy Scripture for which it ought to be believed dependeth not upon the testimony of any man or Church; but wholly upon God (who is truth itself) the Author thereof; therefore it is to be received, because it is the Word of God."

Again, "The whole Councel of God concerning all things necessary for His own Glory, Man's Salvation, Faith and Life is either expressly set down or necessarily contained in the Holy Scripture; unto which nothing at any time is to be added, whether by new Revelation of the Spirit, or traditions of men."

It is simply beyond controversy that the early English Baptists believed in the full authority and integrity of Scripture. Indeed, we could say they believed in the complete inerrancy and infallibility of Scripture.

When we move to the new world, the name of Roger Williams is well-known among seventeenth-century Baptists. Williams is famous for his stand concerning the separation of church and state and the persecution which subsequently resulted. Consider this statement from Williams concerning Scripture:

> I urge that this will of God (for this declaration of what Christ said and did and of all the rest of the Scripture was a Declaration and Revelation of God's Will to his People and to the whole World) this written and revealed will of God I said was the Judge and Decider of all Questions, the tryer of all Spirits, all Religions, all Churches, all Doctrines, all Opinions, all Actions.

Notice once again that Williams refused to limit the authority of Scripture to theological and ethical matters alone. Scripture, according to Williams, was the final arbiter of all matters concerning human existence.

When we move to the eighteenth century, perhaps the most influential Baptist theologian is John Gill of Northamptonshire, England. Gill also was very clear in his statements concerning the authority and inspiration of Scripture, and he too made a clear distinction between the original manuscripts of Scripture, which he referred to as the "original exemplar" and the modern editions. According to Gill, every translation must be checked out by the original editions and thus corrected and amended as necessary. He said, "And if this was not the case, we should have no certain and infallible rule to go by; for it must be all the translations together, or some one of them, not all of them because they agree not in all things: not one; for then the contest would be between one nation and another which it should be, whether English, Dutch, French."

Gill went on to point out that the Roman Catholic Church made a grave mistake in adopting the Latin Vulgate as the official version of Scripture because the Vulgate, he says, "abounds with innumerable errors and mistakes." How could such an unreliable translation be superior to the original manuscripts themselves! He did concede, of course, that our translations are on the whole adequate to produce salvation and to be the basis for the Christian life. Nonetheless, ultimate authority must be sought in the originals.

One of the influential Baptist educators of the nineteenth century was Francis Wayland, who became president of Brown University. His view of Scripture is captured in the following statement:

> There has seemed to me a growing disposition to omit the proof of a revealed truth from revelation, and to attempt the proof from every other source than the Bible. Why should this be? If the Bible be true, why should we ignore its evidence? To do

thus may seem more philosophical, and may be
more pleasing to unregenerate men, but is it really
according to the mind of the Spirit? Do we not
thus practically lead men to the conclusion that
there is a higher authority than the Word of God,
by which it is to be judged and to which its teachings are to be subjected?

Wayland saw clearly that to suggest that the Bible is in
error at any point is to suggest that there is some authority
that is more accurate than Scripture and which can be used
to correct Scripture. This again reflects his fear of the shift
from divine revelation as ultimate authority to one's own rational thoughts as ultimate authority.

One of the most influential leaders of Baptists in the
southern United States in the nineteenth century was John
L. Dagg. He was the first truly "Southern Baptist" theologian. In one of his theological treatises, he says this concerning Scripture: "It cannot be that wicked men conceived
so pure a system; that by every utterance which they made
they condemned their own fraud; and that they have preserved others from perpetrating like iniquity by denuncia-
tions so terrible that the very imagination of them is
unwelcome to the minds of transgressors. The Holy Bible
cannot be the work of unholy deceivers."

He went on to point out that the good men who wrote the
Bible were not liars. Thus, when they claimed that the Bible
is "inspired of God," or "the commandments of the Lord,"
they must be understood to be accurate in those statements.
They were men of integrity. He said, "But a careful examination of the inspired word has not only served to repel the
charge of reconciling the apparent discrepancies, but it is
added new proof that the Scriptures were written by unde-
signing and honest men without any collusion and that there

is perfect harmony in their statements, even when apparently most discordant."

Again Dagg says,

> A candid mind, after contemplating the overpowering evidences of Christianity, would decide that the alleged disagreements of the evangelists cannot furnish a valid objection to the Divine origin of the religion, even if the apparent disagreements could not be harmonized. But patient investigation converts these apparent inconsistencies into undesigned coincidences and finds in the very ground of infidel cavils, a firm foundation for Christian faith.

Notice that Dagg would not support the modern opinion that we should not propose any view of Scripture until we have been able to work out all of the problems and all of the apparent discrepancies in Scripture. Dagg says that we must accept Scripture at face value because of the divine endorsement even though we are currently unable to work out every problem to man's satisfaction.

It is particularly interesting to note the expressed views of early Southern Baptist educators concerning Scripture. When Southern Baptists decided to establish a seminary in 1858, three of the founding professors were John A. Broadus, James P. Boyce, and Basil Manley, Jr. If we can determine their views concerning Scripture, we can ascertain what was the original doctrinal position of the Southern Baptist Theological Seminary.

Consider this statement by Boyce concerning Scripture:

"It must come from God, the source of all our other knowledge. No other could give it, and it is fit that no other should do so.

"It must be suited to our present condition, confirming the truth already known, and teaching what is practically useful to man as a sinner before God.

"It must be secured from all possibility of error, so that its teachings may be relied on with equal, if not greater, confidence than those of reason.

"It must come with authority, claiming and proving its claim to be the word of God, who has the right to command, and to punish those who disobey his command, with authority also, that man may with confidence believe and trust the promises and hopes of pardon and peace it may hold out."

Basil Manley said:

> This full recognition of the human authorship of the Scriptures is of prime importance; for much of the force of the argument against a strict doctrine of Inspiration consists in proving this human authorship of the sacred writings, which we think is undeniable, and then inferring from that their fallibility. "Human, therefore fallible," they say; "fallible, therefore false in some measure." But this favorite line of argument seems to us to be more plausible than powerful. It is a mere assumption that their being human forbids their being also divine; that God cannot so inspire and use a human being as to keep his message free from error; that the human origin, under divine control, necessarily involves either falsity or fallibility. This seems to be perfectly plain: yet this fallacy underlies whole pages of vigorous denunciation and confident appeal.

This argument, which Manley so competently disposes of,

is still current today. How can the Scriptures be the product of human beings and still be inerrant, we are asked. Manley gave the answer which is still as appropriate today as it was then, that is, that God is capable of inspiring a human being so as to keep His message free from error. This is what the church and Baptists have believed historically.

John Broadus, perhaps the most honored name in early Southern Baptist education, prepared a catechism in which we can easily see his view of Scripture.

> Did the inspired writers receive everything by direct revelation? The inspired writers learned many things by observation or inquiry, but they were preserved by the Holy Spirit from error; whether in learning or in writing these things.
>
> What if inspired writers sometimes appear to disagree in their statements? Most cases of apparent disagreement in the inspired writings have been explained, and we may be sure that all could be explained if we had fuller information.
>
> Is this also true when the Bible seems to be in conflict with history or science? Yes, some cases of apparent conflict with history or science have been explained quite recently that were long hard to understand.
>
> Has it been proven that the inspired writers stated anything as true that was not true? No; there is no proof that the inspired writers made any mistake of any kind.

One could scarcely ask for a plainer and more explicit statement of the current position of biblical inerrancy. John Broadus was an inerrantist in the fullest sense of the word.

No review of Baptist history would be complete without

some reference to Charles Haddon Spurgeon (1834-1892), the famous London preacher. He, too, dealt with the charge that if the Bible was written by genuine human beings, then the Bible must contain error. He said,

> One might suppose that believers in Plenary Inspiration were all idiots; for their opponents are most benevolently anxious to remind them of facts which none but half-witted persons could ever forget. Over and over they cry, "But there is a human side to inspiration." Of course there is; there must be the man to be inspired as well as the God to inspire him. Whoever doubted this? The inference which is supposed to be inevitable is—that imperfection is, therefore, to be found in the Bible, since man is imperfect. But the inference is not true. God can come into the nearest union with manhood, and he can use men for his purposes, and yet their acts may not in the least degree stain his purposes with moral obliquity. Even so he can utter his thoughts by men, and those thoughts may not be in the least effected by the natural fallibility of man.

Spurgeon, then, perhaps the greatest of all the modern Baptist preachers, built his ministry unashamedly and absolutely upon the total authority of Holy Scripture.

Not only were the founders of Southern Baptist Seminary believers in biblical inerrancy, but the founder of Southwestern Baptist Seminary was an inerrantist also. B. H. Carroll was as outspoken as Spurgeon in his stand on Scripture. "It has always been a matter of profound surprise to me that anybody should ever question the verbal inspiration of the Bible," he said. "The whole thing had to be written in

words. Words are signs of ideas, and if the words are not inspired, then there is no way of getting at anything in con-
nection with inspiration. . . . What is the object of inspiration? It is to put accurately in human words, ideas from
God. . . . When you hear the silly talk that the Bible 'contains' the word of God and is not the word of God, you hear
a fool's talk. I don't care if he is a Doctor of Divinity, a President of a University covered with medals from universities
of Europe and the United States, it is fool's talk. There can
be no inspiration of the book without the words of the
book."

Carroll also distinguished carefully between the original
manuscripts of Scripture and the copies which we have
today. "Let me say further that only the original text of the
books of the Bible is inspired, not the copy or the translation. Second, the inspiration of the Bible does not mean that
God said and did all that is said and done in the Bible, some
of it the Devil did and said. . . . The inspiration means that
the record of what is said and done is correct. It does not
mean that everything that God did and said is recorded. It
does not mean that everything that is recorded is of equal
importance, but every part of it is necessary to the purpose
of the record, and no part is unimportant. One part is no
more inspired than any other part." Some are saying today
that we have a "progressive inspiration." This idea is foreign
to our Baptist forefathers as shown by this quote from Carroll.

Perhaps the most famous theologian to be associated with
Southwestern Seminary, which B. H. Carroll founded, was
W. T. Conner, who spent some thirty-nine years teaching at
that institution. He retired in 1949. Conner believed that the
Bible was an inspired book and that it was given altogether
by God. Perhaps his most explicit statement is this:

> Dr. Warfield is probably correct when he says that this means that God produced or caused the Scriptures. New Testament writers (and speakers) regard God as the author of Old Testament sayings and teachings (Mark 12:36; John 10:35; Heb. 1:5; 3:7 *et al.*). The Scriptures then, are God's work. He produced the Scriptures. . . .

"Dr. Warfield," of course, was B. B. Warfield, the well-known Princeton theologian of the late nineteenth century, who was a champion of biblical authority and inerrancy. Conner obviously agreed with Warfield.

In these two chapters, then, we have demonstrated that the view of the church down through the centuries, almost without exception, until recent times, has been that the Bible is the authoritative, infallible, inerrant Word of God and that it is our sole source of authority in every given area of human understanding. We have seen that this is true of Baptists as well as other Christians. Perhaps, we could summarize this section by means of a quotation from Kirsopp Lake, late professor of theology and philosophy at Harvard University:

> It is a mistake often made by educated persons who happen to have but little knowledge of historical theology, to suppose that fundamentalism is a new and strange form of thought. It is nothing of the kind. It is the partial and uneducated survival of a theology which was once universally held by all Christians. How many were there, for instance, in Christian churches in the eighteenth century who doubted the infallible inspiration of all Scripture? A few, perhaps, but very few. No, the fundamentalist may be wrong. I think that he is. But it is we

who have departed from the tradition, not he, and
I am sorry for the fate of anyone who tries to argue
with a fundamentalist on the basis of authority.
The Bible and the *corpus theologicum* of the church
are on the fundamentalist's side.[5]

This quote reminds one of the homely story about the
farmer and his wife who were driving to town in their
pickup truck. The farmer was sitting behind the wheel in silence and his wife was sitting against the door, as far from
her husband as she could get, also in silence. After several
miles, the wife said, "Jed, when we were first married, we
didn't sit this far apart."

Jed's reply was, "I ain't moved."

The facts show that current evangelicals who are intent on
maintaining the church's dedication to the full authority of
Scripture are in the mainstream of Christian history and
tradition. It is those who would dilute the authority of
Scripture and who have been polluted by liberal and
neoorthodox theology, who have introduced novelty into
the church. They are the ones who are responsible for the
confusion and divisiveness which have resulted. They are
the ones who have moved.

CHAPTER 5

The Bible Speaks About Itself

"Are we claiming more for the Bible than it claims for itself when we say the Scriptures are inerrant?"

HAVING REVIEWED the historic position of the church concerning biblical authority, we must now turn our attention to what the Bible says about itself. In much of the debate concerning whether the Scripture contains error or not, very little attention is given to what the Bible claims for itself, and especially what Jesus Christ had to say about Scripture. Some today are saying that inerrantists actually claim more for the Bible than the Bible claims for itself. For example, we occasionally hear someone say, "Where does the Bible use the term *inerrant?* If the Bible does not use that term itself, what right do we have to use the term or to urge others to affirm it?" This is a very superficial argument, but it has appeal to some people.

In the first place, we must point out that there are a number of theological terms which Christians have used for centuries which do not occur in Scripture. The word *Trinity* nowhere occurs in Scripture—but the doctrine of the Trinity certainly is clearly taught. The term *hypostatic union*, referring to the union of the divine and human natures of Christ, nowhere appears in Scripture—but the doctrine appears clearly in Scripture. It is a cardinal doctrine of Christianity that Jesus Christ was a perfect, sinless man and genuine deity at the same time, and thus became our perfect sacrifice for sin.

It is not a good argument to claim that because a term does not appear in Scripture it is an invalid term. Whether we use the term *inerrant,* or *infallible,* or *authoritative* or *completely accurate*—whatever term we choose to use— what we really want to know at this point in our investigation is whether or not the Bible claims this for itself. It would be a tragic mistake for us to claim *more* for Scripture than Scripture claims for itself. It would be equally tragic, however, for us to claim *less* for Scripture than Scripture claims for itself.

In reviewing what Scripture says about itself, let us begin with the Old Testament. There are several primary passages from the Pentateuch, and, assuming the Mosaic authorship of these books, these will give us information as to what Moses, the first inspired penman, thought about Scripture.

Exodus is an appropriate place to begin. "And Moses said unto the Lord, O my Lord, I am not eloquent, neither heretofore, nor since thou hast spoken unto thy servant; but I am slow of speech, and of a slow tongue. And the Lord said unto him, Who hath made man's mouth? Or who maketh the dumb, or deaf, or the seeing, or the blind? Have not I, the Lord? Now therefore go, and I will be with thy mouth and teach thee what thou shalt say" (Exodus 4:10–12). This passage states plainly that God gave to Moses the words he was to speak; it thus infers that what He inspired Moses to say and to write was without error.

Further on in the book of Exodus we read, "And the Lord said unto Moses, Write thou these words; for after the tenor of these words I have made a covenant with thee and with Israel" (Exodus 34:27). Once again, Scripture reveals that what Moses wrote was the Word of God, perfect and intact.

In Deuteronomy we find another clear statement. "Ye

shall not add unto the word which I command you, neither shall ye diminish ought from it, that ye may keep the commandments of the Lord your God which I command you" (Deuteronomy 4:2). This is a very explicit statement of God's authority in His revelation.

Finally, Deuteronomy describes how God views a prophet and the importance of communicating the Word of God accurately. "But the prophet, which shall presume to speak a word in my name, which I have not commanded him to speak, or that shall speak in the name of other gods, even that prophet shall die" (Deuteronomy 18:20). Thus, it would have been foolish for Moses to presume to add to or take away from what God had sovereignly commanded him to speak and to write.

It is important to recognize that throughout the Pentateuch there are literally hundreds of references such as, "Thus says the Lord," "The Lord said," and "The Lord spoke." There can be no doubt that Moses claimed to be communicating the actual words of Jehovah God.

Consider Isaiah as a typical representative of the prophetic books. Some twenty times in the book of Isaiah there are claims that his words are the words of the Lord. One of the best illustrations is, "Hear the word of the Lord, ye rulers of Sodom; give ear unto the law of our God, ye people of Gomorrah" (Isaiah 1:10).

Jeremiah, more than one hundred times, states that "The word of the Lord came unto me . . ." or something similar. For example, "To whom the word of the Lord came in the days of Josiah, the son of Amon, king of Judah, in the thirteenth year of his reign. . . . Then the word of the Lord came unto me, saying" (Jeremiah 1:2, 4).

Ezekiel, in more than sixty places, claims that his words are God's words and thus to be received as such. "Moreover, he said unto me, Son of man, all my words that I shall speak unto thee, receive in thine heart, and hear with thine ears. And go, get thee to them of the captivity, unto the children of thy people, and speak unto them, and tell them, Thus said the Lord God; whether they will hear, or whether they will forbear" (Ezekiel 3:10, 11).

Daniel ". . . heard I the voice of his words; and when I heard the voice of his words, then was I in a deep sleep on my face, and my face toward the ground" (Daniel 10:9). Daniel was thus responding to and reporting that which he had heard directly from God Himself.

Each of the twelve minor prophets reflects in an unambiguous and specific way that he was writing the very Word of God as it came to him from Jehovah God Himself. Compare Hosea 1:1, Joel 1:1, Amos 3:1, Obadiah 1, Jonah 1:1, Micah 1:1, Nahum 1:12, Habakkuk 2:2, Zephaniah 1:1, Haggai 1:1, Zechariah 1:1, and Malachi 1:1. The prophets, without doubt, believed that they were recording the very words of God when they spoke or wrote.

In the poetic books, David emerges as the most prominent representative author. The 119th Psalm is a classic expression of the power, the beauty, and the inerrancy of the Word of God. Verse 89 summarizes David's thoughts regarding the accuracy of the Word of God, "Forever, O Lord, thy word is settled in heaven." What a classic statement of David's concept of the Word of God. For those who would like to pursue David's thoughts further, the entire 119th Psalm deals with the truthfulness and the purity of the Word of God.

As we turn to the New Testament to see what it says about Scripture, several key passages are determinative. Paul writes: "All scripture is given by inspiration of God, and is profitable for doctrine, for reproof, for correction, for instruction in righteousness, that the man of God may be perfect, throughly furnished unto all good works" (2 Timothy

3:16, 17). The word translated "given by inspiration of God" (Greek, *theopneustos*) means "God-breathed." *Theos* is the Greek word for God, and *pneustos* is from the word *pneuma,* which means "air," "wind" or "breath." Thus the combination of the two Greek words means "God-breathed." God breathed in (and out) of the sacred writers of Scripture what He wanted them to write, and thus it was God's Word, complete and without error. A holy and perfect God could not conceivably produce error in His Word! The goal was that the man of God might be mature, completely equipped for every good work. Thus, we see that God has "breathed" the Scriptures through man with the result that all Scripture is profitable for us in a practical, day-to-day application. Without the God-breathed Scriptures we would have no absolutes for the Christian life.

When we join these words of Paul with those of Peter we have an excellent view of just what inspiration involves. "Knowing this first, that no prophecy of the scripture is of any private interpretation. For the prophecy came not in old time by the will of man, but holy men of God spake as they were moved by the Holy Ghost" (2 Peter 1:20, 21). Holy men, set apart to God, were "borne along" by God, writing down what God wanted them to say. Peter plainly states that the biblical prophets did not make up Scripture, but that God directed them as to how and what they should communicate. Thus, the accuracy of the revelation would be according to God's standard, which is perfection.

As Peter wrote this passage, I believe he was remembering the Sea of Galilee where he had worked as a fisherman before the Lord's touch upon his life. The Greek word *pneuma* not only means "breath"; it also means "spirit" or "wind." Peter had often sat in that little fishing boat in the middle of the sea, waiting for the *pneuma* to come up and catch his sail and take him back to Capernaum. This was a common experience to Peter. So, by inspiration, he uses this analogy to demonstrate just what happened in the process of inspiration. The holy *pneuma,* the Holy Spirit, the holy "breath" of God, moved the inspired penman along toward the desired destination just as the physical *pneuma,* the wind, moved the sailors in the boat across the sea to the desired destination.

Before we move on to what Jesus said about the Scripture, note briefly three other passages from the New Testament that bear upon this matter. Peter states, "Being born again, not of corruptible seed, but of incorruptible, by the word of God, which liveth and abideth forever. For all flesh is as grass, and all the glory of man as the flower of grass. The grass withereth, and the flower thereof falleth away: but the word of the Lord endureth forever. And this is the word which by the gospel is preached unto you" (1 Peter 1:23–25). How can one read these words and doubt that Peter regarded the spoken and written revelation of God as eternal and perfect?

Another very well-known passage is found in Hebrews. "For the word of God is quick, and powerful, and sharper than any two-edged sword, piercing even to the dividing asunder of soul and spirit, and of the joints and marrow, and is a discerner of the thoughts and intents of the heart" (Hebrews 4:12). These words explain why the Bible is not always a pleasant book to read. People find it hard to read because it is the Word of God and, being alive and active, it penetrates and lays open their innermost being. This supernatural characteristic of the Word of God gives evidence of its divine origin and thus its perfection.

Finally, James declares, "Of his own will begat he us with the word of truth, that we should be a kind of firstfruits of his creatures" (James 1:18). The Word of God was God's means of bringing us to the truth, and it is itself truth (John 17:17).

With this review of the New Testament authors before us, let us look now at what Jesus Himself had to say about Scripture. We will consider Jesus' view of Scripture from several different standpoints. The place for us to begin is to ask: "Did Jesus Himself regard the Scripture as inerrant?" The answer is an unequivocal, "Yes." He believed it to be inerrant. Consider, first of all, how Jesus treated the Old Testament passages as statements of fact. We find throughout the Gospels that Jesus referred to and treated all references to the Old Testament as being factual, chronological, historical material. There seemingly was not a doubt in His mind that what He was referring to was accurate. He spoke of Abel, Noah, Abraham, Moses, Lot, Sodom, Solomon, Jonah, Zechariah, and others, as historical people and places.

Secondly, Jesus used the Old Testament as the final arbiter in all matters of faith and conduct. Whenever He was contending with the scribes and pharisees, Jesus referred to the Word of God as absolutely authoritative. In Matthew 5:17–20, Jesus said, "Think not that I am come to destroy the law, or the prophets: I am not come to destroy, but to fulfill. For verily I say unto you, till heaven and earth pass, one jot or one tittle shall in no wise pass from the law, till all be fulfilled. Whosoever therefore shall break one of these least commandments, and shall teach men so, he shall be called the least in the kingdom of heaven: but whosoever shall do and teach them, the same shall be called great in the kingdom of heaven. For I say unto you, That except your righteousness shall exceed the righteousness of the scribes and Pharisees, ye shall in no case enter into the kingdom of heaven."

Jesus denied that He had any thought of destroying Scripture (as some had charged). The Jewish leaders themselves understood that the Word of God was the final court of appeal, but they had distorted it by adding their own traditions. Compare also Matthew 22:29 and 23:2, 3 for further evidence of Jesus' complete confidence in the Old Testament Scriptures.

Thirdly, Jesus viewed the Old Testament as predicting His own life and ministry. How could this be so without divine inspiration? For example, in John 5:39, Jesus said, "(Ye) search the scriptures; for in them ye think ye have eternal life: and they are they which testify of me." He was, in effect, stating, "You use the scriptures as your source book, and yet you are unable to see the fulfillment of prophecies that relate to me as the Messiah." Other passages that reflect the same understanding are Luke 4:21; 18:31–33; 24:27. Compare also Mark 14:21; Luke 22:37, and Matthew 26:53–56.

Fourthly, Jesus expressly stated the authority of the Old Testament and of His own words. In John 10:35, our Lord said, "If he called them gods, unto whom the word of God came, and the scripture cannot be broken. . . ." Although some have tried to evade the force of those words, it is very obvious that Jesus Christ regarded the words of Holy Scripture as absolutely inviolable!

A second passage for consideration is that found in Mark. "Heaven and earth shall pass away: but my words shall not pass away" (Mark 13:31). It is difficult to conceive of a more explicit statement of the absolute authority of Jesus' words, which words were subsequently recorded in Scripture.

It is important to see that Jesus preauthenticated the New Testament Scriptures; that is, by His own statements He marked out the apostolic writings as fully inspired *before they were written.* Consider what He says in John 14:26— "But the Comforter, which is the Holy Ghost, whom the Father will send in my name, he shall teach you all things, and bring all things to your remembrance, whatsoever I have said unto you." In John 16:12–14, Jesus declares, "I have yet many things to say unto you, but ye cannot bear them now. Howbeit when he, the Spirit of truth, is come, he will guide you into all truth; for he shall not speak of himself; but whatsoever he shall hear, that shall he speak: and he will shew you things to come. He shall glorify me: for he shall receive of mine, and shall shew it unto you." Christ thus makes provision for the Scripture which was yet to be written, that is, the New Testament. Matthew 16:18, 19 also refers to the authority of Christ Himself which was to be entrusted to the apostles so that they would be able to carry out the divinely-appointed responsibilities. "And I say also unto thee, That thou art Peter, and upon this rock I will build my church; and the gates of hell shall not prevail against it. And I will give unto thee the keys of the kingdom of heaven: and whatsoever thou shalt bind on earth shall be bound in heaven: and whatsoever thou shalt loose on earth shall be loosed in heaven."

Having reviewed what the Lord Jesus Christ Himself said about Scripture, a crucial question emerges that must be answered. Can evangelicals be truly such and deny Jesus' own expressed view of Scripture? If Jesus believed in the inerrancy of Scripture (and He certainly did), how can presumed evangelicals speak in terms of Jesus as Lord and reject His view of Scripture? This is, perhaps, the most important consideration that we must face in the entire discussion of inerrancy. Southern Baptists, in particular, make a great deal out of the fact that Jesus is Lord. If Jesus is Lord, then, by definition, that means that He is Lord of all of life. He is Lord in every area and avenue of life. It is a contradiction in terms for us to acknowledge Jesus as Lord, on the one hand, and then reject His lordship in some particular area. The point is this: if Jesus really believed in biblical inerrancy, then we need to believe in biblical inerrancy, be-

cause He said so and He is Lord! Even if there are some
seeming discrepancies which we have not yet been able to
work out, if Jesus said the Bible is inerrant and if He firmly
believed it Himself, then we must believe it or else reject His
authority and His lordship.

This logically brings up the question of what is called
"circular reasoning." Someone will undoubtedly say that,
philosophically, we are reasoning in a circle. We are making
a big thing about the fact that Jesus believed in biblical inerrancy, and thus we must believe in biblical inerrancy because He did. But, all that we know about Jesus' position on
Scripture is contained in Scripture. Therefore, they say, we
have to presume biblical inerrancy in the first place in order
to know what Jesus said about anything. Then, we take
what He presumably said about Scripture and use it to urge
others to believe in inerrancy as well. In other words, we
could be accused of using the Bible to prove the Bible.

Many evangelicals have confronted this problem in a very
satisfactory manner, and I will briefly outline the most effective approach, that is, the principles of historiography.
How do historians determine whether an ancient document
is genuine or bogus? Over the years they have developed a
measuring stick that can be applied to any historical document to determine whether its contents are to be accepted as
fact or rejected as fiction. *Such a test will not prove scriptural
inerrancy,* but it will give us an acceptable indication that the
New Testament documents really do reflect actual people,
events, and statements, arising from the first century A.D.

Briefly, the point is this: we can escape the problem of
circular reasoning by moving back for a moment from the
whole question of biblical inspiration and inerrancy and in-
quiring about the essential accuracy of Scripture, based
solely upon the principles of historical investigation and
criticism. When any document comes to us from some point

in history, the historian who works with the document must have some means of evaluating and determining its reliability and its integrity. The New Testament documents, and particularly the Gospels, are no different. They can be subjected to the tests of historical criticism. Essentially these tests are two—external and internal.

The external test deals with the genuineness of the document itself: Does it actually come from the period represented? Is it a forgery? Do we have an original document or is this an accurate copy of the original? This is basically the problem of textual criticism.

Basically, the internal test covers such matters as the primary witness's *ability* to tell the truth. What about competence, degree of attention, the danger of leading or loaded questions? Is the primary witness *willing* to tell the truth. Was there bias? Who are the intended hearers? What literary style is used? What about the laws and conventions of the time in which the document was written? Is the primary witness accurately reported with regard to the detail under examination? Is there independent corroboration?

Applying these tests to the New Testament documents we can establish the basic veracity of our Lord's statements, apart from theological considerations. We are then on solid ground in taking the statements of Jesus concerning biblical accuracy and regarding them as essentially accurate. And, if they are essentially accurate, and He did indeed declare that Scripture is inerrant, is totally reliable, and cannot be broken, then it is our final court of appeal. By this particular methodology we can escape the problem of circular reasoning and come right back to the major point. If Jesus really did regard the Bible as being inerrant and infallible, how can any person who calls himself a Christian take any other view?

To support this a little further, there is widespread agree-

ment among prominent *liberal* theologians that Jesus did, in
fact, believe in the full authority of the Scripture. For example, H. J. Cadbury of Harvard Divinity School, F. C. Grant
and John Knox of Union Theological Seminary, Adolf
Harnack and Rudolf Bultmann, two of the most famous of
the German theologians, all agreed that Jesus, without
question, believed as the rabbis of His day believed, that
Scripture is totally without error, totally authoritative and
reliable.

To a man, all of these liberal theologians believed that
Jesus was mistaken, but they nonetheless admitted that such
was His belief. If this is what Jesus believed, how can we
believe anything differently? The liberal mind can claim
that Jesus is wrong, but we evangelicals cannot. Therefore,
we are put in this very demanding position of either affirm-
ing biblical inerrancy as Jesus did or else contradicting the
very authority of the One whom we call Lord.

However, should we not be "inductive" in our approach?
There are those within the evangelical camp who are saying
that the scholarly thing to do would be to maintain an inductive approach to the evidence. What they mean is this:
let us not go off the deep end, let us not go off half-cocked
and state dogmatically that Scripture is inerrant, when, as a
matter of fact, we have not checked it out completely to determine if it is inerrant. In other words, what we ought to say
is that we believe that it *may* be inerrant but we are waiting
until all the data are analyzed before we can make that as a
final, dogmatic statement.

What this means is that as long as there is a single apparent discrepancy in the biblical account, we cannot defi-
nitely and dogmatically say that Scripture is inerrant,
because it just might prove otherwise. Therefore, scientifically, inductively, we should be cautious and "scholarly"

and wait until all the evidence is in before we come up with the final pronouncement.

That simply will not do! If we wait until all the "evidence" is in, we will wait until the Second Coming of Christ! By then, it will be too late for us to affirm our belief in the inerrancy of Scripture. We say again, the main reason we accept the inerrancy of Scripture is not because we have all of the problems worked out, not because we can reconcile every difficulty, but simply because Jesus Himself said so and we believe Him because Jesus is Lord!

There is one other consideration we must examine. That is the area of God's holiness. Essentially, the question arises, "Can a holy God inspire an errant Word?" If the Bible is considered to be the Word of God in any meaningful sense, can a holy, perfect, righteous God inspire something which is imperfect, unholy, and full of errors, imperfections, and false information? Whatever God does, He does perfectly. That is the answer to this basic question. The fact that God has used human beings does not mean that He cannot produce a perfect Word. Utilizing their imperfections, their personalities, their vocabulary and literary style, He nonetheless has produced something perfect, which will not lead astray and will not deceive those who depend upon it.

CHAPTER 6

Biblical Authority: What We Do and Don't Mean

"The doctrine of inspiration simply says that God the Holy Spirit superintended, He overruled men's imperfections, and did not allow those imperfections to intrude into the Scripture which they wrote."

WHEN WE TALK about biblical authority and inspiration, what do we mean? The more liberal thinkers have circulated accusations depicting conservative Christians as ignorant and foolish in their views on this subject. They have muddied the waters with accusations which, by and large, are "straw men," verbal tools to discredit what they do not accept or perhaps do not understand. This is the old game of ridiculing your opponent in a debate and intimidating him rather than honestly facing up to his declarations. At this point it is necessary to destroy some of these "straw men" that have been unjustly set up and frequently used. To do that, we need first of all to say what biblical inspiration *does not* mean.

Mechanical Dictation

It does not mean mechanical dictation, that is, that God dictated the material to the writers as a businessman would to his secretary. I do not know of any modern evangelical scholar who believes in mechanical dictation. Yet this "straw man" is constantly thrown up against conservative Christians. In spite of many denials, in spite of all of the evidence to the contrary, opponents are still using this old, moth-eaten argument. It needs to be nailed down one more time. WE DO NOT BELIEVE IN MECHANICAL DICTATION. The definition of inspiration which reflects the classic understanding of the church is this: God so supernaturally directed the writers of Scripture that without waiving their human intelligence, literary style or personal feeling, His complete and coherent message to man was recorded with perfect accuracy, the very words of the original Scripture bearing the authority of divine authorship. God used the human intelligence, the literary style, the personal feelings of each author. He did not override them. He did not force material through a reluctant penman. He supernaturally prepared the penman.

Some people in B. B. Warfield's day (the late nineteenth century) were saying that inspiration might be compared with sunlight shining through a stained glass window into a cathedral. They claimed that just as the stained glass colors the light and changes its hue, so God's truth, when it passes through imperfect man, is bound to emerge differently from what it was originally. Therefore, they said, we cannot eliminate this aspect of humanity in Scripture.

Warfield, in his customary logical fashion, took their illustration and turned it around. Of course, we could think of the truth of God as light coming from Him, passing through a stained glass window into a cathedral. But he asked: did it ever occur to you that the architect who designed the cathedral designed that stained glass in precisely such a manner as to give the exact hue to the light that the window does give? Therefore, rather than the light being discolored, it is colored precisely as the architect wished it to be colored, to give just the proper tone and balance to the interior lighting of the cathedral. So, Warfield proceeded to apply this analogy. When God decided to bring Paul's epistles into being, for example,

> He was not reduced to the necessity of going down to earth and painfully scrutinizing the men He found there, seeking anxiously for the one who, on the whole, promised best for His purpose, then violently forcing the material He wished to express through him, against his natural bent and with as little loss from his recalcitrant characteristics as possible. Nothing of the sort took place. If God wished to give His people a series of letters like Paul's, He prepared a Paul to write them. The Paul he brought to the task was a Paul who spontaneously would write just such letters.[6]

This old "straw man" about mechanical dictation should be rejected once more and, hopefully, laid to rest.

Only the Originals Are Inspired

Secondly, *biblical inspiration does not mean that the translations or editions or versions are inspired—only the original manuscripts, the* autographa. This has also caused a lot of furor today. There are those who are saying that this does not really make sense, that since we do not have the original manuscripts it makes no difference whether the originals were inspired or not. It is a cop-out, they say, to claim that scribal errors have been made, for example, when we do not have the originals to prove it.

Some critics also assert that the idea of inerrancy as applying only to the *autographa* is a very recent view and that it never occurred to the ancients. Listen to Warfield again:

> This is a rather serious arraignment of the common sense of the whole series of preceding generations. Are we to believe that no man until our wonderful nineteenth century ever had acumen enough to detect a printer's error or to realize the liability of hand-copied manuscripts to occasional corruption? Are we really to believe that the happy possessors of the so-called "wicked Bible" held "thou shalt commit adultery" to be as divinely inerrant as the genuine text of the seventh commandment, on the ground that the inerrancy of the original autographs of the Holy Scriptures must not be asserted as distinguished from the Holy Scriptures which we now possess? Of course, every man of common sense, from the beginning of the world, has recognized the difference between the genuine text and the errors of transmission and has attached his confidence to the former in rejection of the latter.[7]

Warfield goes on to say:

> Everybody knows that no book was ever printed, much less hand-copied, into which some errors did not intrude in the process. As we do not hold the author responsible for these in an ordinary book, neither ought we to hold God responsible for them in this extraordinary book which we call the Bible.[8]

Such ought to consider this statement from Augustine:

I do not doubt that their authors [the biblical au-
thors] therein made no mistake and set forth nothing that might mislead. If, in one of these books, I
stumble across something that seems opposed to
the truth, I have no hesitation in saying that either
my copy is faulty or the translator has not fully
grasped what was said, or else I myself have not
fully understood.[9]

Notice that as far back as Augustine, there was clear understanding of the difference between the original manu-
script and the copy or edition which he might have in his
hand. If there was an error, it might be in the copy, but it
would not be in the original.

Another question arises. Why would God allow the originals to perish if they are so important? We certainly do not
know for sure, but Thomas Grantham, an early Baptist
mentioned previously, had a noteworthy comment.
Grantham said that perhaps God allowed the *autographa* to
perish because, if they had survived, they might have fallen
into unscrupulous hands and be altered so as to produce
heresy; then there would be no way to restore the original
readings. Whereas, under the present circumstances, nobody
anywhere has the lock on all of the existing manuscripts of
Scripture. Some of the earliest, most reliable ones are in the
Vatican library, some are in the British Museum, others are
in museums and universities scattered around the United
States. But altogether, through the process of textual criticism, we have essentially restored the *autographa.*

Whether this is the reason why we do not possess the originals or not, this at least makes good sense and certainly answers the question as to why we make so much of the
originals when, as a matter of fact, we do not have them.

The Human Element

Thirdly, *biblical inspiration does not eliminate the human element in Scripture.* The human element is there, in vocabulary, in style, in the way people say things, the way they think. But the point is that God superintended the process so that no error intruded into the text. Some today are saying that unless we rule out the human aspect of Scripture altogether, we have to agree that the biblical writers were omniscient and sinless. This is so, they say, because if there were any flaw in their knowledge or character, they would obviously have written Scripture that was flawed and, in some ways, obviously wrong. But that is not necessarily true at all. The doctrine of inspiration simply says that God the Holy Spirit superintended, He overruled their particular imperfections, and did not allow these imperfections to intrude into the Scripture which they wrote.

For example, it is quite likely that the Apostle Paul believed that the earth was flat, and that if one sailed through the Pillars of Hercules he would fall off the side eventually. We do not know this, but it is quite likely that such was his belief. Some are shocked at this, but I think that it is probably true. The point is that it was not necessary for God to inform the Apostle Paul concerning every aspect of human knowledge in order that he might write Scripture. Paul was never called upon to comment on the shape of the earth. Therefore, it does not make any difference what he believed about it. It is not necessary for the writers of Scripture to understand Einsteinian physics in order to be able to write accurate Scripture. What is important is that they not be allowed to introduce error into what they did write, and that is what we believe happened through divine inspiration.

Figures of Speech

Fourthly, *biblical inspiration does not eliminate figures of speech.* This is where the word *literal* is somewhat unfortunate. When we talk about literal interpretation, some people take that to mean that we believe all the Bible is to be interpreted in a very plastic, literalistic fashion, ruling out all figures of speech. This is absurd, but it is a common misconception. There are twenty to thirty different kinds of figures of speech found in Scripture, and it is simply ludicrous to say that we do not recognize these. As a matter of fact, we need to emphasize that it is just as destructive of biblical truth to take a figurative passage literally as it is to take a literal passage figuratively or allegorically. Either will destroy the intended meaning of Scripture.

Let me give several illustrations of this point. The Roman Catholic doctrine of transubstantiation (that the elements in the Lord's Supper literally become the body of Christ and the blood of Christ) is a grossly literal misunderstanding of a simple metaphor. When Jesus declared, "This is my body . . . this is the new testament in my blood . . ." He was using a metaphor which simply declares that the elements of the Lord's Supper represent His body and blood. By taking literally what was intended to be metaphorical we find great misinterpretation and misuse of a simple truth revealed by our Lord.

Another illustration of this is found in Matthew 5:29, 30. In these verses Jesus declares, "And if thy right eye offend thee, pluck it out, and cast it from thee: for it is profitable for thee that one of thy members should perish, and not that thy whole body should be cast into hell. And if thy right hand offend thee, cut it off, and cast it from thee: for it is profitable for thee that one of thy members should perish, and not that thy whole body should be cast into hell." The cutting off of the hand and the plucking out of the eye are prime examples of hyperbole, that is, an intentional exaggeration given for effect. The literal understanding of these statements by some in church history has led to self-mutilation. Again, the teaching is in the form of hyperbole and is not to be taken literally of the destruction of these parts of the body. The obvious meaning is that no sacrifice is too great to avoid hell.

Approximations and Imprecise Speech

Fifthly, *inspiration does not eliminate approximations and loose quotations.* We do this in common speech. Why should we not recognize that the biblical writers do the same? We frequently say that Jesus Christ was on this earth two thousand years ago. At other times, we say He was here nineteen hundred years ago. Both of these are acceptable approximations, and neither is to be regarded as an error, because they are not intended to be exact.

We may say, for example, that the Bible teaches that God loved the world so much that He gave Jesus Christ His only Son to save us and if we believe on Him we will not perish. That is an acceptable approximation of John 3:16, but it is not a verbatim quotation. It is acceptable in our vernacular today. It was also acceptable in the day of the biblical writers, and it does not mislead or deceive the reader.

Exact Duplication Not Required

Sixthly, *inspiration does not demand exact duplication in parallel passages*—such as in the Gospel accounts. Even when there is an apparent discrepancy, we should be cautious and patient. The assumed or presumed discrepancies may well result from our incomplete understanding. Kenneth Kantzer, former editor of *Christianity Today*, gives an interesting illustration of this from his own experience. A friend of his was rushed into the hospital in critical condition. One person told Dr. Kantzer that his friend was on foot and had been struck by an automobile, injured, and taken to the hospital. Someone else called him very shortly thereafter and said that his friend was riding in an automobile, that there had been an accident, and that his friend was injured and taken to the hospital. Dr. Kantzer did not know which one to believe. On the face of it, the reports appeared to be contradictory. But he later found out that both reports were true. His friend had indeed been hit as a pedestrian and placed in an ambulance, but while en route to the hospital, the ambulance was involved in an accident and the friend had sustained further injuries in this second accident. That may be a bit unusual, but it demonstrates the fact that two partial accounts may both be accurate, even though they seem to be contradictory. When all the information is in, they may both prove to be right. Since we do not know precisely what took place on the occasions when Jesus spoke and did certain things, we must be very, very cautious about presuming so-called "error" just because of differences in the accounts. It is more likely that when all the facts are known to us eventually, we will find that they are perfectly compatible and simply give different aspects of the event.

Grammatical Conformity

Seventhly, *inspiration does not mean grammatical and syntactical conformity.* Today, because of our schooling, we tend to think that people who do not observe certain so-called "rules of grammar" are departing into unacceptable speech. But we must be reminded that grammar is not a set of rules which we must obey. Grammar simply describes how a society has spoken and written in a particular generation and thus communicated effectively. Ultimately, what we are trying to do in speech is to communicate thought. If the thought is communicated adequately and accurately, the individual idiosyncrasies of grammar and syntax are not to be considered as errors, but simply as peculiarities of the individual writer, even as we have today. For example, executive newsletters rarely contain a complete sentence. Everything is presented in staccato style—short statements such as "Boom ahead," "Inflation down," and so forth. These newsletters speak in a language which businessmen understand. They are designed this way to communicate as much information as possible in a limited amount of space. This is not incorrect, nor does it confuse or mislead. Similarly, the fact that Paul begins Ephesians 3 with a sentence that has no verb is a peculiarity of his style; it does not constitute an error.

What Do We Mean by Inspiration?

Let us now look on the positive side. By inspiration we mean that the Bible is accurate in all that it says and that it will not deceive its readers theologically, historically, chronologically, geographically, or scientifically. In other words, it may contain approximations, it may use figures of speech, it may use the common language of the day, but whatever it says, the Bible says it accurately.

Of course, the Bible is *not* a textbook on science. Of course, it is *not* a textbook on history. It is important to note that it is *not even* a textbook on theology! But whatever it says about *any* of these is correct, and no one will ever be deceived or led into error by believing what the Bible says. That is the crucial point.

Finally, let me say a word about terminology. Sometimes

we speak of *verbal inspiration.* We simply mean that, in the original autographs, every word is inspired of God. Sometimes we speak of *plenary* inspiration. Plenary means that all the words are inspired—every one of them! Ecclesiastes is just as inspired as Romans. The Song of Solomon is just as inspired as the Gospel of John. All of it is God-breathed. *Infallible* is literally defined in the dictionary as that which cannot deceive or that which cannot lead astray or be deceived. *Inerrant* means without error. It is important to understand that ALL OF THESE TERMS ESSENTIALLY SAY THE SAME THING. The terminology is flexible. The terminology can even be dispensed with. No one word is essential and everyone is not required to use the same words. Choose *true,* or *accurate,* or whatever word conveys the same idea.

I certainly have no problem with or objection to "truth without any mixture of error" as stated in our Baptist Faith and Message, except that some within our convention have distorted that phrase to the point where it is virtually meaningless. Of course, they can do that with every other term also. They can take the term *inerrant* and say that it means inerrant *in purpose,* that God accomplishes what He wants to accomplish through the Bible inerrantly, even though there may be factual errors in Scripture.

Those who criticize conservative Christians for using all of this terminology should consider the reason why we have to keep coining new terms to describe our position. It is because others keep usurping the old terms and twisting them into something totally different from their original meaning. I would have no objection to simply speaking of the inspiration of Scripture, except that the term has been used in such diverse ways for the last two centuries by those who no longer believe in the historical doctrine, that we have had to come to a more definitive terminology.

Take the word *Christian,* for example. Why should that not be sufficient? I am a Christian. Why should I have to say that I am an evangelical Christian? Why should I have to say that I am a born-again Christian? Those terms are actually tautological. They should not have to be used. They are redundant. But we feel a necessity to use those terms because the term *Christian* has now been usurped by those who are not really Christians. Therefore, we try to sharpen our terms in order to make absolutely clear what we mean.

The same thing is true of inspiration. We keep adding terms such as *inerrant,* or *infallible,* or *verbal,* or *plenary* because the simple term *inspiration* has long since been taken over by those who do not really believe in historic inspiration at all. We keep coming up with new adjectives in an attempt to preserve the original definition. But the terms are relatively unimportant. It is most emphatically not a problem of semantics. It is the concept that is important. We need to understand that, whatever terminology we use, the issue before us today is *not interpretation,* it is *not transmission,* it is *accuracy.* In other words, it is not a question of interpretation, but it is a question of what the Bible *is* rather than what the Bible *says.* It is *not literal versus figurative.* It is *not that which we have versus that which we do not have.* That is not the point. The point is whether or not we can trust the Bible. Is it trustworthy in all that it says, not just in areas of theology? Is it our ultimate authority in every area of knowledge?

Historically, the Christian church has said YES, it can be trusted. It is accurate. There are those today, however, who are saying that it is *not* altogether trustworthy and accurate. It is trustworthy, they say, in matters of faith and conduct, in matters of theology and morals, but not necessarily in matters of science, history, chronology, or geography. That position leads to the problems we talked about in Chapter

One. If we say it is not trustworthy in some of these areas, we have shifted our base of authority, and there is no intrinsic reason why we should maintain that it is authoritative in theology either. Scripture does not teach that it is authoritative in some areas and not in others. It teaches that it is authoritative in all that it says. That is what Jesus said. Therefore, there is no logic in assuming that it is authoritative only in some areas and not in others.

We must emphasize that, according to the clear inference of Scripture itself, of Jesus, and of the church fathers, the Bible is either reliable altogether or else it is not necessarily reliable at all and thus may be suspect at any point. Who is to say where it is reliable and where it is not? The modern answer is that the Holy Spirit will guide us, but that is nothing more or less than existential philosophy. That is nothing more than sheer mysticism. That cuts the very ground out from under the ultimate authority of Scripture, because, as we have already seen, mysticism (for our purposes) is a form of rationalism, and it now becomes a basis of authority above Scripture. It means that man's mind is the grid through which all data and all phenomena must pass. It leads to an entirely different form of Christianity from that known historically and biblically.

Thus we come back to the "tragic step" with which we began. What is the answer? Is there any hope of salvaging historic Christian orthodoxy without some theological absolutes?

CHAPTER 7

The Southern Baptist Convention and Authority: What To Do Now?

"Can evangelism and missions continue at a strong pace when the doctrinal foundations begin to crumble? The answer to that is no! Historically we have strong evidence to that effect. There is no historical example of a church or denomination which became more and more zealous for genuine biblical evangelism and missions while at the same time it became less biblical in its theology and moved away from the authority of Scripture."

CONSERVATIVE, Bible-oriented Southern Baptists have awakened to what is happening. We are still basically a solidly conservative people who are committed to the Bible as the totally reliable Word of God. We realize now that forces are at work among us which are contrary to that basic posture. We have not chosen to demand immediate termination of personnel from convention institutions, nor have we endeavored to dictate a "creed" to which all Southern Baptists must subscribe. Although this has been the accusation, this is not in fact the case. What is the case is that we are demanding the right to be heard as contributing, cooperating, and loyal Southern Baptists. There is no "take-over agenda" by which certain people are being promoted to key positions with definite and specific instructions for actions on their part. Instead, there is an attempt to get representative people on the various boards and agencies of our Southern Baptist Convention so that the diversity of convictions, so publicized by some, may truly be represented in decisions and policies throughout our convention.

Some have accused conservatives of trying to destroy academic freedom and excellence. The implication being, of course, that to be a conservative Christian is to be ignorant and opposed to real education and free inquiry. Yet, the opposite is actually true. In many classrooms, for instance, the textbooks used and the position of the professor give no place at all for traditional biblical views. Evolution is taught as being biblical, and Creation often ridiculed. Higher critical assumptions such as the documentary hypothesis of the Pentateuch are often taught as the only proper approach, while the "old fashioned" conviction of Mosaic authorship is either totally ignored or ridiculed. This is the height of anti-intellectualism. Under the guise of free inquiry, such inquiry is actually discouraged. Many of us do not feel that we can remain silent while professors use tenure and academic freedom as licenses to intimidate students and to ridicule beliefs which they bring to the classroom from their home churches. True inquiry would lead to the honest and fair presentation of all material so that the student, being adequately trained to discern all of the elements in a given matter, can make his own judgments.

For this reason I have constantly called for balance in teaching and in the representation on our faculties and boards. The cry of "wolf" which is going up across this convention is often because of a desire to disallow such balance. If Southern Baptists are truly a diverse people, then the solidly conservative aspects of that diversity must have opportunity to be seen in our organization at the points of real opportunity for input, instruction, and decision making. We must not be afraid of questions and we certainly must cease to make those who raise questions feel that they have committed a cardinal sin.

We have many fine teachers, administrators, and trustees across our Southern Baptist Convention. I thank the Lord for them. There are faculties, however, at some of our educational institutions, which grant only token acknowledgment to conservative views, at best. In some classrooms, when students reflect the beliefs of the churches that nurtured them, they are ridiculed for those beliefs. This is not to be tolerated. No longer can we expect thousands of churches to contribute to institutions that contradict what the churches believe and stand for in their communities. We must allow for a balance to be demonstrated and the classroom must truly become a place of free inquiry. Where that is so I applaud and rejoice. Where that is not so I urge such balance to be instituted.

It is one thing to point up the problem and quite another to point toward a solution. Earlier we mentioned the decline of once-great evangelical denominations. I have before me a copy of an editorial in the December 2, 1981, *Baptist Standard.* It quotes Adon Taft, a correspondent for the Religious News Service, who wrote about the decline of foreign missionaries sent overseas in the last twenty years by major American denominations. During this twenty-year period, the decline in the number of foreign missionaries was 79 percent in the Episcopal Church, 70 percent in the Lutheran Church in America, 70 percent in the United Presbyterian Church, 68 percent in the United Church of Christ, 66 percent in the Christian Church, and 46 percent in the United Methodist Church. This demonstrates the fact that when biblical authority as a base of theology begins to decline, missions and evangelism also decline very quickly. When a person begins to doubt the authority of Scripture, or, to put it another way, when he substitutes human reason for divine revelation, this inevitably cuts the very nerve of evangelism and missions in the biblical sense.

So we ask, can evangelism and missions continue at a strong pace when the doctrinal foundations begin to crumble? The answer to that is NO! Historically we have strong evidence to that effect. There is no example in history of a church or a denomination which became more and more zealous for genuine biblical evangelism and missions while at the same time becoming less biblical in its theology and moving away from the authority of Scripture. These two concepts are antithetical. The more biblical one is, the more he is interested in that which is biblical, that is, missions and evangelism. The less biblical one becomes, the more interested he becomes in the "social gospel." Therefore the argument concerning the continuation of missions and evangelism is a false argument; the exact opposite is actually true.

One thing further needs to be emphasized. Those who are still talking about missions and evangelism as being the great glue holding our convention together need to define exactly what they mean by missions and evangelism. They would say that it has to do with "winning people to Jesus," and many would stop at that point and suggest that such a goal is sufficient and that we can all work together for that purpose. Sadly, such is not necessarily the case. Harry Emerson Fosdick, one of the most outspoken liberals of the twentieth century in the United States, wrote a book entitled, *The Meaning of Faith* in which he speaks a great deal about winning people to Christ and bringing them to faith. Yet, Fosdick did not believe in any of the great doctrines of the Christian faith. He did not believe in the deity of Christ, the bodily resurrection, eternal punishment, or judgment. Therefore, though he used much of the terminology of biblical theology, he substituted entirely different meanings for these terms.

We have people today in our convention who are talking about evangelism and about "winning people to Jesus," but they do not mean the same thing that the Bible means, and they do not mean the same thing that Southern Baptists historically have believed. Historically, evangelism has been the attempt to bring men to personal faith in Jesus Christ the Son of God, Deity in human flesh, the incarnate Second Person of the Trinity, born of the virgin Mary, One who lived a sinless life, who died a substitutionary, vicarious atonement for our sins, who was raised bodily from the dead, who ascended bodily into heaven and who is going to return bodily and physically to this earth. By placing one's faith in that Person and accepting Him as Lord and Savior and committing one's self to Him as a disciple, a believer receives the imputed righteousness of Jesus Christ and is declared righteous; that is, he is justified by God's grace through faith.

This is the gospel that Southern Baptists historically have preached. This is what we have meant historically by "winning people to Jesus." Today, however, there are those who are using this same terminology but who mean something quite different. In the most extreme case, some simply mean that we need to come and follow the teachings of Jesus, that we need to undertake to follow the ethical example of Jesus. These would be out-and-out liberals. But even within the neoorthodox, existentialist camp there are those who would define evangelism as bringing people to Jesus in the sense of committing themselves to Him as their leader, as their guide—even as their Lord, in a lesser sense. But what they mean is that we simply should follow Him, that we should do as He did, that we should love as He loved, that we should forgive as He forgave, that we should live according to the principles of the Sermon on the Mount, that we should make Jesus the one who is our exalted teacher and even our commander. But there is little or nothing said about His vicarious atonement for our sins. They speak of the fact that Jesus died for us but they do not really mean that He died in our place as an actual sin offering to the Father.

We need to get beneath the terminology—that is, such terms as inerrancy, authoritative, infallibility, verbal plenary inspiration. We need to come to the point where we can define exactly what we mean by the gospel. When we come to that level we are going to find that there is a very significant shift away from the biblical gospel. THIS IS WHERE THE REAL PROBLEM LIES. IT IS NOT IN TERMINOLOGY. IT IS NOT IN SEMANTICS. It is in the basic definition of the gospel of Jesus Christ, and we cannot join hands and go forward effectively in evangelism and missions unless we are agreed as to precisely what evangelism and missions are. What are we asking people to do? What is it that Jesus Christ claims? What is it that He commands, that He demands of those who would be His disciples? Until we have worked through this, it is superficial to speak of joining hands and going forward in the great work of evangelism and missions. I am very much afraid that we do not agree with some of our brethren as to what evangelism and missions are.

Some years ago, the national director of evangelism for a major Baptist convention said that, for them, evangelism had taken on a different sense from that which the previous generation had known. He said that they once thought of evangelism as "saving souls." Now, he said, we believe that evangelism has to do with improving the plight of man on this planet, and such practical things as jobs, housing, discrimination, and equality. That is evangelism today to us, he said. The term was the same, but the concept was widely different.

But, some cry, what about our cherished doctrine of the priesthood of the believer? They are using the term, priesthood of the believer, to mean that an individual Baptist has the right to believe anything he wants to believe, and that no other Baptist has a right to say he is wrong, criticize him, or in any way interfere with his beliefs or with his teaching of those beliefs in our Baptist institutions. That, of course, is a complete distortion of the doctrine of the priesthood of the believer. According to Scripture, the doctrine of the priesthood of the believer teaches that all believers in Jesus Christ have immediate, direct access to the Father through Jesus Christ, the only Mediator, and that we do not need any other man, or any other being of any kind, to intercede for us. Those who misuse this term are invoking a doctrine that means a great deal in Baptist circles, making it apply to something to which it does not apply. The priesthood of the believer has nothing to do with the concept of what a person may believe and teach and still be regarded as a "good Southern Baptist." Baptists must continue to be people of the Book. Certainly each individual can go to God for himself and interpret the Bible for himself, but this cannot be a license to promote nonbiblical views without restraint in our cooperative efforts.

"Soul competency" is also the cry of many and it, too, is being used improperly. The historic Baptist principle of soul competency is that we do not need an authoritative church to tell us exactly what we must believe and what we must do. The Roman Catholic Church, for example, claims to be the infallible interpreter of the Scriptures for Roman Catholics. The church establishes canon law and thus presumably determines the life-style of Roman Catholics. The Free Church movement, of which the Baptists are a part historically, has always believed that we need no such authoritative proclamation from an ecclesiastical authority. We are capable of being directed personally from the Scriptures without the intermediate step of an authoritative church. That is a tremendously valuable concept, and we should defend it to the death. But, again, it has little or nothing to do with the current controversy. Today people are saying, "I am a Southern Baptist. I am a Christian. Thus, I am competent to interpret Scripture for myself. And if I interpret Scripture in such a way that I do not see the deity of Christ, and I do not see the substitutionary atonement, and I do not see the bodily resurrection, then I am simply applying the concept of soul competency. That is the way I understand it; that is the way I interpret it, and no other Southern Baptist has the right to tell me I am wrong. He has no right to impinge upon my freedom of expression, *even in a Baptist classroom.* If he tries to impinge on me, he is violating my basic rights as a Southern Baptist Christian."

This sounds very appealing, and it is intimidating to many, but it is a distortion of the concept. The precious Baptist concept of soul competency has nothing to do with the denial of plain scriptural teaching. The very idea that early Baptists would have denied the plain teaching of Scripture is completely beyond imagination. This concept has to do with the difference between Scripture as authority and the church as authority. As I said earlier, there are three great bases of authority: reason, ecclesiastical authority, and divine revelation. Soul competency has to do with the fact that we are subject to divine revelation as our ultimate authority and not to ecclesiastical fiat. It has nothing to do with the shift from divine revelation to human reason. And yet, that is the way people are applying it today. It is being used today as a subterfuge for apostasy, rather than as a justification for elevating divine revelation above church authority.

But, we are frequently told, all Southern Baptists believe the Bible. It is in the interpretation of the Bible where we differ, and we have every right to differ there. This sounds very plausible and reasonable, but it does not deal with the real problem.

No one in his right mind wants to exercise some dictatorial authority over the legitimate bounds of interpretation. Bible-believing Christians have long differed as to the exact nature of the millennium, for example. Will Jesus Christ return before or after the Great Tribulation? Does man consist of two parts or three? Does man inherit his soul by natural generation, as he does his body, or does God create it immediately? Is God's elective purpose for man conditional or unconditional? And the list goes on. Most Christians would agree that there is sufficient doubt about these matters that extreme dogmatism is inappropriate. Certainly these matters should not be allowed to become a barrier to fellowship and cooperative effort.

The present crisis, however, goes much deeper than this. "Interpretation," in many instances, has become a convenient cover for a denial of scriptural authority. Let me give you some examples. 1 Kings 6:1 says that 480 years elapsed between the Exodus from Egypt and the fourth year of Solomon's reign in Israel. If this chronology is taken seriously as a real historical statement, the Exodus occurred in the middle of the fifteenth century B.C. (that is ca. 1450–1440 B.C.). This was indeed the chronology used by almost all Old Testament scholars for most of church history. In recent times, however, some highly debatable interpretations of certain archaeological data have led many scholars to abandon this "early date" of the Exodus and opt for the "late date," that is, the thirteenth century B.C. Here is a clear example of the shift in one's ultimate authority base. If Scripture is ultimate authority, the early date must be regarded as valid, because Scripture is absolutely unambiguous here. If something else is ultimate authority (in this case archaeology), the Scripture must be "corrected." The issue is not ultimately interpretation; it is authority.

Another example. Scripture teaches that Adam was created directly by God as the first man, and that he was created from inorganic matter ("dust"). Darwinian evolution teaches that man evolved from lower forms of organic life by natural processes. How can one imagine a clearer contrast? Yet, many professing Christians, including some Southern Baptists, hold to the position of "theistic evolution," that is, that God really did create man, but that He did it by means of the evolutionary process. The Bible tells us Who and Why, we are told, while modern science tells us How. But, again, this simply won't do for an honest interpreter. There is no way that the Bible can be actually "interpreted" in any legitimate sense to teach theistic evolution. It must actually be denied, even though many are reluctant to admit that such is the case. Again, we have a problem of authority. The theistic evolutionist believes modern evolutionary science to be more authoritative than the "primitive" concepts of Scripture, thus revealing that he is operating from the base of rationalism rather than revelation.

Such "interpretations" can eventually cut the very heart out of biblical Christianity. Some theologians "interpret" the Bible as not teaching the deity of Christ, as not teaching the bodily resurrection of Christ, as not teaching the lostness of man and his everlasting doom without Christ, as not teaching salvation by grace through faith apart from any merit of his own. These are not merely varying interpretations within the pale of historic Christianity. These are denials of the faith under the guise of "interpretation." There must be some control on this sort of thing or else it makes absolutely no difference what we believe about anything biblical, so long as we simply "love Jesus," whatever that may mean.

The sanctity of academic freedom is also being used against conservative Christians today. We are told that the "fundamentalists" are not really interested in genuine education; they are intent instead on pushing a narrow indoctrination. Furthermore, those in academia never tire of suggesting that "creedal interference" from constituents may well jeopardize institutional accreditation and drive away the most competent faculty members.

Again, academic freedom is a valuable concept when correctly perceived, but it is not a blank check for faculty members to teach anything they please. Even the classic 1940 statement on academic freedom from the American Association of University Professors recognized that church-related institutions might legitimately limit such freedom so as not to undermine the very purposes of the institution. Subsequent commentary has tended to play down this provision, but it was in the original statement (*AAUP Policy Documents and Reports,* 1951 Edition, p. 2). I recognize that the Southern Baptist Convention only operates seminaries, and that our colleges and universities are administered by the state conventions. Nevertheless, state conventions are composed of Southern Baptists. What I have said applies there also, but would have to be dealt with on a state convention level.

What is not widely recognized, however, is that there is generally a much wider breadth of learning in conservative institutions than in liberal institutions. If you would care to research this point, here are some suggestions. Check the bibliographies in conservative textbooks and note how many books are listed from other theological perspectives.

Then check the more liberal textbooks and note the total absence of any references to conservative works. The same phenomenon is to be seen in course syllabi handed out in the classrooms. Check the catalogs of theological institutions and note the course offerings. Most conservative institutions will include courses in "The Theology of Karl Barth," or "The Theology of Rudolf Bultmann." But do the liberal institutions offer courses in "The Theology of Charles Hodge," or "The Theology of B. B. Warfield"? You will look in vain. Speak to students who have attended the various institutions and ask them how much time is given to opposing viewpoints and options. If there is any "narrow indoctrination" going on, it is going on in the liberal institutions far more than in the conservative ones.

Again, why is academic freedom only for nonconservatives? Why is it that genuine evangelicals who believe in the total inerrancy of Scripture are not given even token consideration for faculty openings in many of our Southern Baptist seminaries and colleges? It surely isn't because of their lack of academic credentials, because many of them have advanced degrees at least as prestigious as those who are appointed. The fact is that their theological conservatism simply is not welcome on many of our campuses. Where then is academic freedom in these cases? If the concept is valid, it must be applied to all of us and not just to those of a more liberal orientation.

What is the ultimate answer to all of this? No one in his right mind wants to start on some sort of wild-eyed witch hunt whereby we charge into our schools and agencies and lop off heads right and left. I have steadfastly maintained that we must work within the system to express ourselves, AND I CONTINUE TO MAINTAIN THAT TODAY! I cringe at the thought of something being done that is destructive and precipitous. Usually many innocent people are hurt in such attempts to "clean house." I have never called for personnel to be fired or eliminated. However, the presentation at all levels in our classrooms and materials must be balanced if we are to expect continued strong support for our cooperative efforts. You cannot tell people that it is none of their business what goes on in institutions that are funded from common gifts, and expect those people to continue their strong financial support.

Can we bring forth any concrete suggestions that make sense and that can reasonably be applied without some sort of unbridled fanaticism? The answer is YES! The answer, I believe, lies in the determination of theological parameters. In other words, we need to have a consensus among Southern Baptists as to the irreducible minimum theology that a person must subscribe to in order to be acceptable as a professor at one of our schools, or as a worker, writer, or policymaker in one of our agencies. I would strongly suggest that the parameters be reduced to the most basic fundamentals, beyond which a person really ceases to affirm the Christian faith. It goes without elaboration that we must view the Bible as the unquestioned Word of God to mankind.

I would suggest that the first basic parameter be the undiminished Deity and the genuine humanity of Jesus Christ in one person—the hypostatic union.

Secondly, I would suggest the doctrine of the substitutionary atonement of Christ, that He actually died in our place, in our stead, and that He suffered a penal judgment from the Father on behalf of us, for our sins. Man is eternally lost apart from Christ, thus such atonement is absolutely necessary.

Thirdly, I would suggest that we require a belief in the literal, bodily resurrection of Jesus Christ from the grave, a literal, bodily ascension into heaven and a literal, bodily return of Jesus Christ to the earth. Eschatological views would not be required. Whether or not one held to a view of premillennialism or amillennialism, for instance, should not be a test in any way. That is a matter of interpretation which has always been widely diverse among Southern Baptists.

Fourthly, I would suggest that we require a person to believe in the doctrine of justification by God's grace through faith.

Obviously, there are a number of important doctrines which I would like to see subscribed to, but I submit that these mentioned constitute the irreducible minimum. If a person does not subscribe to these doctrines, then he really is not an evangelical Christian; he is not a biblical Christian.

Could we not then agree, as a convention, that this is the irreducible minimum to which a person must subscribe in order to be a teacher, a policymaker, a leader in our convention? This is not to say that we should rule those who refuse out of the convention as a whole. We do not want to get to the point where we start telling churches who can pastor their churches. That is not Baptistic. The church can call anyone it chooses as its pastor, but if a person wants to teach in a Southern Baptist institution or wants to write curriculum or have a policymaking role in one of our agencies, then it seems reasonable that he or she be asked to subscribe to these biblical parameters.

We have strong biblical support for establishing such parameters. 1 Timothy 3 and other passages reveal a different standard for church membership than for leadership positions. So it is entirely proper for us to establish minimum standards of biblical parameters. In addition, we might want to add some Southern Baptist distinctives for those who would assume teaching positions in our seminaries which have the primary responsibility in training our ministers. For instance, we might want to include such things as belief in baptism by immersion of believers, regenerate church membership, and eternal security among standards for such leadership positions. These, too, are biblical doctrines and have been firmly held by Southern Baptists from the beginning of our convention. No one needs to subscribe to these additional distinctives to be a biblical Christian, but just to be a Southern Baptist Christian with teaching or leadership responsibilities which include writing or policy-making. Surely it is neither narrow nor doctrinaire to require that a professor in a Southern Baptist seminary accept baptism by immersion of believers only. I do not suggest that we have some who do not believe this, but only to illustrate that there are some Southern Baptist distinctives that we must not lose. As Southern Baptists we do have some distinctive understandings of New Testament teachings. Diversity does not mean giving these up.

If Southern Baptists are not willing to set forth some specific parameters then we must resign ourselves to the fact that anything goes, and there should be no further criticism of anybody who believes, teaches, or advocates anything. If there are no parameters, then the sky is the limit and we can have Unitarians, Mormons, Jehovah's Witnesses and others teaching in our schools. Nobody would have a right to raise any question, because, if there are no parameters, then there are no limitations. If there are some parameters, then we need to decide what they are, define them, and set them forth. It seems to me that this is the only way this process can go forward.

Some may say, "We have the Baptist Faith and Message and that is sufficient." I agree that it should be sufficient. Yet, in recent days we have seen this statement so twisted and misinterpreted that one can claim allegiance to it and not really mean what the statement obviously means. We must be more specific, and in the most minimum way state our parameters. Several questions could be asked of leaders and teachers, and their honest answers would reveal where they stand. As it is now, a straight answer is difficult to get. If there is any response at all, it is something like this: "Well, it depends on what you mean by that term. . . ." Any time a person answers in such a manner, you know that person has reservations and does not believe the way an affirmative answer would designate. It is time for us to have some simple answers to some very simple questions and to expect that the integrity of our personnel is such that they would meet these minimal parameters, or work elsewhere.

I would suggest that the Southern Baptist Convention, at one of its annual meetings, delegate to someone the authority to appoint a blue ribbon committee which would draw up such a set of parameters, and then present it for convention debate and possible adoption. Perhaps some other process would be more effective. But unless Southern Baptists continue to stand for something other than simply cooperation with a program, in some political or social sense, there is no question that Southern Baptists will go down the same road that once-great denominations have taken. It will not be long before we will be simply a shadow, a caricature, of what we once were—perhaps one of the most effective witnesses for Jesus Christ in church history. This would be an unspeakable tragedy. Although we do not want to do anything intemperate, fanatical or ill-advised, we also do not want to be guilty of doing nothing and thus allowing the whole matter to get infinitely worse by default.

I love our Southern Baptist Convention. I am a third generation Southern Baptist preacher. Every church I have ever served has generously supported the Cooperative Program. As far as I know we have always increased our gifts to the Cooperative Program every year I have pastored a Southern

Baptist church. I was led to Jesus Christ in a Southern Baptist church and educated at Southern Baptist schools. My entire life is wrapped up in Jesus Christ through this convention. We must do something to maintain the strength and aggressive ministry that has historically characterized this convention. We cannot allow the cry of "diversity" to intimidate us. Proper balance, within stated parameters, must be demonstrated and nurtured if our historical stance as Southern Baptists is to be preserved. These pages may not hold a valid answer, but they are my attempt to help the convention I love through days of struggle into victory for our Lord Jesus Christ.

A Personal Word to Southern Baptist Pastors and Their People

"Our supreme loyalty will be to Jesus Christ as our Lord and Savior. Such loyalty will cause us to love the Bible, know the Bible, obey the Bible. We who declare our strong commitment to God's Word must become people who read it, memorize it, study it, appropriate it and live it."

"TAKE HEED UNTO thyself and unto the doctrine; continue in them; for in doing this thou shalt both save thyself and them that hear thee" (1 Timothy 4:16).

"For which cause I also suffer these things; nevertheless, I am not ashamed; for I know whom I have believed and am persuaded that he is able to keep that which I have committed unto him against that day. Hold fast the form of sound words, which thou hast heard of me, in faith and love which is in Christ Jesus. That good thing which was committed unto thee keep by the Holy Ghost, who dwelleth in us" (2 Timothy 1:12–14).

This is an edited version of Dr. Draper's Presidential Address to the Southern Baptist Convention in Pittsburgh, Pa., in 1983.

"Thou, therefore, my son, be strong in the grace that is in Christ Jesus. And the things that thou hast heard from me among many witnesses, the same commit thou to faithful men, who shall be able to teach others also" (2 Timothy 2:1, 2).

Early in 1983 the Southern Baptist Convention passed the 14 million mark in membership. In addition, over 1.5 million people are members of churches connected with Southern Baptist foreign missions. We now serve in all fifty states and in one hundred countries. Total baptisms in 1982 in the U.S. and on foreign fields was 552,398. Without doubt, the Southern Baptist Convention has been on the cutting edge of missions and evangelism for the many years of its existence. We have led the battalions of those carrying the light of the gospel, seeing the darkness of unbelief retreat. We have taken seriously the challenge of sacred Scripture to reproduce New Testament Christianity in our age through the power of the Holy Spirit. Wherever we have gone we have been used of the Holy Spirit to change the face of the world for the better.

We have been that special kind of people because we are a people of DEEP BELIEFS AND CONVICTIONS. We have made a firm commitment to biblical principles—principles for which our forefathers even dared to die. We carry these beliefs in the spirit of Christ and in obedience to the Word of God.

Only people with such commitment can become God's change agents in a sin-cursed world. Weak convictions and shallow beliefs have never impacted the world. We have been used of God to impact the world because of our firm commitment to our beliefs. We shall continue to make an ever increasing impact as long as we hold consciously and firmly to these basic, foundational beliefs.

The basis of these beliefs is the Word of God. From every

section of our Southern Baptist Convention recently—in books, speeches, news releases, and through many other means—we have heard affirmations of our commitment to the Bible as the final authority for Southern Baptists. In this conviction concerning the Word of God we must stand united. Our only hope for strength and vitality in our denomination is our renewed and continued commitment to this divinely inspired, uniquely transmitted, carefully preserved and totally reliable book. These great beliefs that have so characterized Southern Baptists are cherished biblical truths.

I want to review with you a few of these deep beliefs that have been so characteristic of Southern Baptists over the years. This list is not exhaustive; each truth includes many others.

The Full Humanity and Full Deity of Jesus Christ

This is known as the doctrine of the hypostatic union— the union of the two natures of Christ, Deity and humanity (from the Greek *úpóstasis,* nature, essence). Jesus Christ is undiminished Deity and genuine humanity, joined in one person, forever. He is God's perfect man and man's perfect God.

"For in Him dwelleth all the fullness of the Godhead bodily" (Colossians 2:9). Jesus is *not* "all of God that a human being can contain." He is *not* "the most God-like man who ever lived." He is *not* "the best demonstration of God that man has ever seen." HE IS GOD ALMIGHTY IN HUMAN FLESH. He is undiminished Deity!

Jesus is also genuine humanity. He was *not* the heavenly phantom of Docetic Gnosticism. John refuted this charge when he said, ". . . every spirit that does not confess that Jesus Christ has come in the flesh is not of God. And this is the spirit of the Antichrist, which you have heard was coming, and is now already in the world" (1 John 4:3). He was (and is) a real, genuine, flesh-and-blood human being. He is undiminished Deity and humanity. Herschel Hobbs declared, "It is true that Jesus Christ was God. But even more wonderful, God became Jesus of Nazareth! . . . When God would reveal His law He did so through a man, Moses. But when He revealed His grace He became a man, Jesus Christ."[10]

This is vitally important for us. Concerning salvation: Only a *man* could die for other men. Only the God-man's death could have infinite value. Concerning priesthood: Only a *man* could be a priest (Hebrews 5:1). Only the God-man could be an eternal high priest (Hebrews 7:17–28).

W. T. Conner declared:

> But to speak as if the Christ of John were a supernaturalistic prodigy without divine powers or qualities—this is wholly to misinterpret both John and the Synoptics. The Christ of both is both human and divine . . . while he is God's eternal Son, he is genuine man. He did not cease to be divine but he did become human.[11]

The belief in the bodily resurrection of Jesus Christ is vital. We must believe this in order to be saved according to Romans 10:9–10. The bodily resurrection authenticated Christ's claims, for He was ". . . declared to be the Son of God with power, according to the spirit of holiness, by the resurrection from the dead" (Romans 1:4). It demonstrates God's acceptance of the atonement, for He ". . . was delivered up for our offenses, and was raised again for our justification" (Romans 4:25). It assures us of our own resurrection, for Jesus declared ". . . because I live, ye shall live also" (John 14:19). His bodily resurrection assures us of needed power, for the Apostle Paul declared "that I may know him, and the power of his resurrection . . ." (Philippians 3:10). Further, the bodily resurrection assures the world of the certainty of judgment. "Because he hath appointed a day, in which he will judge the world in righteousness by that man whom he hath ordained; concerning which he hath given assurance unto all men, in that he hath raised him from the dead" (Acts 17:31).

Liberal and neoorthodox theologians have long denied the truth of the bodily resurrection. Paul Tillich called it, "absurdity compounded into blasphemy."[12] Rudolf Bultmann taught that the "resurrection" took place in *heilsgeschichte* ("holy history") and not in actual space and time.[13]

Against this backdrop of heresy, Southern Baptists have firmly held to the truth of the full Deity and full humanity of Jesus Christ which includes deep belief in His physical, bodily resurrection. W. D. Nowlin, a great Southern Baptist leader early in this century, wrote, "It is accepted by all true Christians that the Death, Burial and Resurrection of Christ are fundamental facts of the Christian religion."[14]

The Lostness of Mankind

The Word of God teaches that man is *dead* in trespasses and sins (Ephesians 2:1) and is totally incapable of doing anything to help himself apart from the convicting ministry of the Holy Spirit (John 16:8–11). This applies to all men (Romans 3:23; 5:12). When Adam sinned, man fell from his state of innocence and fellowship with God. Now sin and misery are the inheritance of all mankind. Mankind is now alienated from God. We are all strangers from God (Ephesians 2:12). By sin we are enslaved to Satan. He enslaves the understanding and binds us in ignorance. He enslaves the will. Man does not refuse evil—he willingly sins. Every area of man's life is polluted. Sin takes possession of the heart and makes it desperately corrupt (Jeremiah 17:9). Like a cancer, sin permeates the whole being of man and man is LOST, destined for misery, emptiness, frustration, and despair.

Mankind is *lost* regarding the provision of God. *Lost*— every part of his nature is tainted with sin. *Lost*—his spirit is darkened (Ephesians 4:17, 18). *Lost*—his body is diseased and death-ridden (Romans 7:24). *Lost*— under wrath and judgment (John 5:28, 29), under God's condemnation (Galatians 3:10). *Lost*—bound for eternal hell and separation from God (Matthew 25:41). *Eternal* in Matthew 25:46 applies to the life of the redeemed *and* to the punishment of the lost. There is no evidence in Scripture that hell is anything less than eternal. Without a hell, evangelism is meaningless, but evangelism is what Christianity is all about. We are constantly admonished throughout the Bible to reach the lost.

L. R. Scarborough said:

> The most gigantic undertaking God has laid out for Christian men is to lead lost souls to Jesus Christ. The salvation of the world cost God more, and requires more from man, than any other movement in human or divine history. . . . The divine obligation of soul-winning rests without exception upon every child of God. . . . Regeneration demands reproduction in kind. The fruit of a Christian is another Christian. . . . Some men are divinely called to preach to a lost world; some women are called to give life and power in home and foreign fields to teach a redeeming gospel. Every Christian is called in the hour of salvation to witness for Jesus Christ. Nothing in heaven or on

earth can excuse him from it. God gives no fur-
loughs from this heaven-born obligation. Not ignorance, or poverty, or environment, or difficulties
of any kind—nothing—can exempt or excuse any
child of God from its pressing daily importance.[15]

Scarborough went on to say:

A compassionless Christianity drifts into ceremo-
nialism and formalism. Our greatest need now is
for a compassionate leadership in the Christian
movements of the world. Every niche of this lost
world needs the ministry of a fired soul, burning
and shining with the zeal and conviction of a con-
quering gospel. Spiritual dry rot is worse for the
churches of Jesus Christ than the plagues were for
Egypt and the simooms are for the Sahara. Many a
minister is on a treadmill, marking time, drying
up, not earning his salt, because he has no passion
for souls and no power for effective service. May
our God kindle holy fires of evangelism in all
churches and pulpits where such is needed![16]

Roland Q. Leavell wrote, "Do you honestly believe that
unbelievers are actually lost, tragically lost, eternally lost?
The Scripture could not be plainer in declaring the frightful
lostness of those who refuse Christ. . . .

"Souls! Souls! Souls! was the burden of Christ's heart. His
love for men never allowed him to lose consciousness of the
fact that men by the multitudes were lost."[17]

Substitutionary Atonement

This great truth simply defined is that Jesus Christ died
on Calvary as an innocent sacrifice *in the place of* guilty sin-

ners. His death actually propitiated or satisfied the holiness of God and was necessary that eternal justice might be accomplished. He was not a martyr, or an example of God's love. He was our SUBSTITUTE.

"Purge out, therefore, the old leaven, that ye may be a new lump, as ye are unleavened. For even Christ, our passover, is sacrificed for us" (1 Corinthians 5:7).

"Who his own self bore our sins in his own body on the tree, that we, being dead to sins, should live unto righteousness; by whose stripes ye were healed" (1 Peter 2:24).

"For Christ also hath once suffered for sins, the just for the unjust, that he might bring us to God, being put to death in the flesh but quickened by the Spirit" (1 Peter 3:18).

"For he hath made him, who knew no sin, to be sin for us, that we might become the righteousness of God in him" (2 Corinthians 5:21).

"Surely he hath borne our griefs, and carried our sorrows; yet we did esteem him stricken, smitten of God, and afflicted. But he was wounded for our transgressions, he was bruised for our iniquities; the chastisement of our peace was upon him, and with his stripes we are healed. All we like sheep have gone astray; we have turned every one to his own way, and the Lord hath laid on him the iniquity of us all" (Isaiah 53:4–6).

W. T. Conner declared:

> The death of Christ was a vicarious work. It was substitutionary. He did something for us which we could not do for ourselves. The matter can be simply stated as follows: On account of our sin the sentence of death came upon us. Jesus had no sin. Yet death came to him. It came on account of our sins and on behalf of us. He took upon himself the sentence of death that was due to us. By bearing that sentence he sets us free. This is what is meant

when it is said that we are redeemed with the blood of Jesus (1 Peter 1:19). The blood stands for the life which he freely gave up for us.[18]

J. L. Dagg wrote, "All propitiatory sacrifices involve the idea of substitution. The animal offered represented the offerer, and bore his sins, which were confessed, over its head. So Christ bore our sins, our iniquities being laid on him."[19]

This is perhaps the most hated of all the doctrines of biblical Christianity by the liberal theologians. The late Bishop G. Bromley Oxnam, president of the World Council of Churches, said, "I would rather go to hell than go to heaven on the back of another man."

Our Southern Baptist heritage is firmly committed to the substitutionary atonement of Jesus Christ. W. D. Nowlin declared emphatically, "The price is the Blood of Jesus Christ."[20]

E. Y. Mullins writes of the fact of substitution:

> The New Testament teaching does not leave the matter doubtful. . . . The idea of substitution is inseparable from the facts, and various passages of Scripture declare it. . . . What he did for us we could not do for ourselves. We could not, as sinful, die an atoning death for the sinful. As victims of the sin-death principle reigning in humanity, we could not become its conqueror. We could not break the power of death and annul the law of sin and death. But Christ did both these things for us. This is substitution.[21]

J. L. Dagg writes:

> In being made under the law, Christ became our substitute; and his obedience and sufferings are

placed to our account, as if we had personally obeyed and suffered, to the full satisfaction of the law. . . . Our sins were imputed to Christ when he died for them; and his righteousness is imputed to us when we receive eternal life through him. He was treated as if he had personally committed the sins which were laid on him; and all who believe in him are treated as if they had personally rendered that satisfaction to the law which was rendered by his obedience and sufferings.[22]

Justification by God's Grace through Faith

Justification is that act of God whereby He declares a guilty sinner to be righteous, not on the basis of any intrinsic quality in the sinner, nor on the basis of anything which the sinner may produce in the way of conduct, but solely on the basis of the sinner's trust in Jesus Christ. Paul's great statement is, "Therefore, we conclude that a man is justified by faith without [literally, "apart from"] the deeds of the law" (Romans 3:28).

Grace means unmerited favor. God is obliged to save no one. It is of His grace that He saves anyone. Sinners have *no claim* on a Holy God, but God has *graciously* determined to save those who believe on Jesus Christ.

Faith, which is essentially synonymous with repentance, is the *only* prerequisite for salvation. "Faith only" was the great rallying cry of the Reformation. *Faith plus anything*— baptism, sacraments, good works—is the Galatian heresy and falls under the *anathema* of Galatians 1:8, 9.

Dagg says:

The doctrine that salvation is of grace, is taught in the sacred Scriptures with great clearness. . . . Salvation is entirely of grace. . . . That salvation is entirely of divine grace, may be argued from the condition in which the gospel finds mankind. We are justly condemned, totally depraved, and, in ourselves, perfectly helpless.[23]

Justification is the very foundation of Christianity. An error here destroys the whole structure of our Christian faith. Justification is mercy surging from the heart of free grace. The basis of our justification is Christ's atoning work on the cross. By faith we receive this justification. E. Y. Mullins declares, "Justification belongs to the great series of spiritual blessings which come to us in and through Christ. And faith is the condition of them all."[24]

Holiness of Life

God has called the redeemed to holy living (1 Peter 2:9). Paul declares that we are saved by grace, through faith, but *unto* good works (Ephesians 2:10). "Nevertheless, the foundation of God standeth sure, having this seal, The Lord knoweth them that are his; and, Let everyone that nameth the name of Christ depart from iniquity" (2 Timothy 2:19). We are called to holy living. Peter states, "But, as he who hath called you is holy, so be ye holy in all manner of conversation" (1 Peter 1:15).

Dr. Scarborough wrote:

Those who handle the vessels of the Lord must have pure hearts and clean hands. Holiness unto the Lord must be on the skirts of God's spiritual priests today. "Consecrate yourselves today to the Lord" (Exodus 32:29) is God's command to those who would win souls to him.[25]

It is God's purpose to make us holy. To do that we must see sin as God sees it. He calls sin "an abomination" (Deuteronomy 7:25). God has no mixture of sin in Him. *Sin has no mixture of good in it!* Sin turns good into evil. It defaces, debases, and destroys all that is good. Sin is called a "cursed thing" (Deuteronomy 7:26). It is against God, unlike God. If sin were to triumph, God would no longer be God. We must see the tragic nature of sin if we are to become holy. Southern Baptists have always held that it is the great design of God in this world for us to become holy people. Holiness sets us apart from the world and allows us to approach God in boldness.

We must be light in the darkness, salt in the earth. We must again become people of prayer and fasting with holy lives. I call upon Southern Baptists today to return to the practice of a regular time of prayer and fasting. We must return to confessing sins and beseeching God for real revival. Our churches must once again become examples of holiness and commitment in our communities. Such a call to prayer and fasting need not be complicated or need it be a media event. I am speaking about simple communication among God's people which will recognize that our only hope in the world is a mighty, sweeping revival of God.

The Urgency of Mission

God has sent us on a mission of great urgency. This world is filled with billions of people who are dying at the rate of five thousand every hour! The majority of them are dying without Jesus Christ. We have the GOOD NEWS of redemption and we must declare it to every person in this world. That is the goal of BOLD MISSION THRUST. But BOLD MISSION is not just a Southern Baptist slogan—it is a *divine mandate!* We must witness to every individual in this world—*we must!*

"So thou, O son of man, I have set thee a watchman unto the house of Israel; therefore, you shall hear the word at my mouth, and warn them from me. When I say unto the wicked, O wicked man, thou shalt surely die; if thou dost not speak to warn the wicked from his way, that wicked man shall die in his iniquity, but his blood will I require at your hand" (Ezekiel 33:7, 8).

"And this gospel of the kingdom shall be preached in all the world for a witness unto all nations; and then shall the end come" (Matthew 24:14).

Jesus declared, "I must work the works of him that sent me, while it is day; the night cometh, when no man can work" (John 9:4).

My wife and I awakened a neighbor some years ago and led the family to safety from a burning house. The need was urgent. Death was imminent. We had to act. Such is the case in this world. Lost mankind is dying without the Savior and we must preach the gospel to every person. "Thus it is written, and thus it behooved Christ to suffer, and to rise from the dead the third day; and that repentance and remission of sins should be preached in his name among all nations, beginning at Jerusalem. And ye are witnesses of these things" (Luke 24:46–48).

In discussing Acts 1:7, 8, W. O. Carver said, "Our whole, sole duty is to witness for Jesus and our first concern must be to receive power to do this effectively."[26] The urgency of mission has no boundaries. That which we cannot do directly, we may do through others. That is why we cooperate together—to make possible the preaching of the gospel everywhere in the world.

W. T. Conner states, "Our mission is to bear witness to Christ from Jerusalem to the uttermost part of the earth.

Any form of Christianity that does not have throbbing through it a mighty missionary and evangelistic impulse is a degenerate form."[27]

Any theology or supposed belief that does not thrust us into all the world to witness and preach is heresy! It is not possible to please God with intellectual assent only. We must "do the truth" (1 John 1:6). Conner continues, "Missions and evangelism, therefore, are not incidental or secondary in the Christian life; they are of the very essence of Christianity. And any form of so-called Christianity that does not practice the spread of the gospel among men thereby proves itself false in its claim."[28]

James Franklin Love said, "The minister who does not covet souls courts guilt. He cannot be innocent before God and indifferent to a lost humanity."[29]

What kind of people will such beliefs produce? If we honestly and conscientiously believe these truths we will reflect in our lives their reality. We will be absolutely loyal to our Lord Jesus Christ. We will recognize that by His shed blood we have been reconciled to God. We will live in the awareness that this reconciliation came by His grace and through no merit of our own. Our supreme loyalty will be to Him as our Lord and Savior. Such loyalty will cause us to love the Bible, know the Bible, obey the Bible. We who declare our strong commitment to God's Word must become people who read it, memorize it, study it, appropriate it, and live it.

Southern Baptists are people of deep beliefs. Those beliefs must be expressed in all we do through every church, every agency and institution, every organization of Southern Baptist life—indeed in each of us individually if we are to continue to be torchbearers in a sin-darkened world. We have been and will continue to be light-bearing, evangelistic, mission-minded people of God in this great day of opportunity. To these truths I reaffirm my commitment and challenge each Southern Baptist to join me in that commitment.

Let us press on in our task. Satan will oppose. Skeptics will accuse. The apathetic will yawn indifferently. The intellectual will lose himself in rhetoric. The activist will grind on relentlessly. The liturgical will carry on precisely. The organizational man will keep oiling the machinery. But in the midst of it all, committed Southern Baptists will march on, together, hand in hand, heart in heart, to the beat of the heavenly drummer, declaring to this lost world, "that God was in Christ reconciling the world unto himself, not imputing their trespasses unto them, and hath committed unto us the word of reconciliation. Now, then, we are ambassadors for Christ, as though God did beseech you by us; we pray you in Christ's stead, be ye reconciled to God" (2 Corinthians 5:19, 20).

We are on a BOLD MISSION FOR OUR LORD and we will succeed for His glory, in His power, by His Spirit.

Notes

1. George C. Bedell, Leo Sandon, Jr., and Charles T. Wellborn, *Religion in America,* 2nd edition (New York: Macmillan, 1982), p. 246.
2. George E. Ladd, *The New Testament and Criticism* (Grand Rapids: Wm. B. Eerdmans, 1967), p. 40.
3. Ibid.
4. "The Challenge of Secularism to Christian Higher Education," a pamphlet published by the Education Commission of the Southern Baptist Convention.
5. Kirsopp Lake, *The Religion of Yesterday and Tomorrow* (Boston: Houghton Mifflin, 1926), p. 26.
6. B. B. Warfield, *The Inspiration and Authority of the Bible,* 2nd edition (Phillipsburg, N.J.: Presbyterian & Reformed, 1948), p. 101.
7. "Inerrancy of the Original Autographs," *Selected Shorter Writings of Benjamin B. Warfield,* Vol. 2, edited by John Meeter (Phillipsburg, N.J.: Presbyterian & Reformed, 1973), p. 585.
8. Ibid., p. 582.
9. George Duncan Barry, *The Inspiration and Authority of Holy Scripture* (New York: Macmillan, 1919), p. 140.
10. Herschel H. Hobbs, *The Baptist Faith and Message* (Nashville: Convention, 1971), p. 41.
11. W. T. Conner, *The Faith of the New Testament* (Nashville: Broadman, 1940), p. 391.

12. Paul Tillich, *Systematic Theology,* Vol. 2 (Digswell Place: James Nisbet, 1957), p. 180.
13. Rudolf Bultmann, *Kerygma and Myth,* ed. H. W. Bartsch (London: SPCK, 1957), pp. 39–42.
14. W. D. Nowlin, *Fundamentals of the Faith* (Nashville: Sunday School Board of the Southern Baptist Convention, 1922), p. 197.
15. L. R. Scarborough, *With Christ After the Lost* (Nashville: Broadman, 1952), pp. 2, 3.
16. Ibid., p. 31.
17. Roland Q. Leavell, *Evangelism, Christ's Imperative Commission* (Nashville: Broadman, 1951), p. 17.
18. W. T. Conner, *Christian Doctrine* (Nashville: Broadman, 1937), pp. 175, 176.
19. J. L. Dagg, *Manual of Theology* (Harrisonburg, Va.: Gano, 1982), p. 211.
20. Nowlin, *Fundamentals,* p. 223.
21. E. Y. Mullins, *The Christian Religion in Its Doctrinal Expression* (Philadelphia: Judson, 1917), p. 325.
22. Dagg, *Manual,* p. 269.
23. Ibid., p. 259.
24. Mullins, *The Christian Religion,* p. 393.
25. Scarborough, *With Christ,* pp. 12, 13.
26. W. O. Carver, *The Acts of the Apostles* (Nashville: Broadman, 1916), p. 14.
27. W. T. Conner, *The Gospel of Redemption* (Nashville: Broadman, 1945), pp. 220, 221.
28. Ibid., p. 221.
29. James F. Love, *The Unique Message and the Universal Mission of Christianity* (New York: Fleming H. Revell, 1910), p. 240.